"Glain Roberts-McCabe masterfully taps into more than twenty years of executive coaching and support to provide a sublime blueprint towards people-first leadership. *The Grassroots Leadership Revolution* delivers a practical yet thorough outline that will positively enrich how you build community."

DAN PONTEFRACT, bestselling author of *Open to Think* and *The Purpose Effect*

"*The Grassroots Leadership Revolution* is a genuine gift to anyone who needs a roadmap for improving themselves as a leader. Glain Roberts-McCabe lays out the needed structure and specific action steps that will actually pay off. The essence of the book is how to build an effective community that will provide mutual support and benefit. In our Stakeholder-Centered Coaching practice, we help leaders do the same by enlisting carefully chosen stakeholders who have a 'stake' in the leader's success."

FRANK WAGNER, partner, Marshall Goldsmith Group and co-founder of Stakeholder-Centred Coaching

"*The Grassroots Leadership Revolution* is a concise and easy to follow roadmap to build your own peer coaching system. As a Roundtable alumnus, I can say that the process can be incredibly powerful to unlocking performance IF you choose to put in the work and leverage the insights it can provide. Glain's leadership wisdom is well-placed throughout this book and her trademark straight-shooting style will make sure you know exactly what you need to do next. A great read and a great tool for the leadership toolbox."

TREVOR LEWINGTON, CEO—Economic Development Lethbridge and Mayor—Village of Stirling

"In *The Grassroots Leadership Revolution*, Glain Roberts-McCabe presents a compelling and practical roadmap for leaders to support one another to raise their collective effectiveness and success. No matter where you are in your career as a leader, you will find many gems in this book that will propel you to the next level."

DR. VINCE MOLINARO, founder and CEO of Leadership Contract Inc., *New York Times* bestselling author, and leadership adviser to boards and C-Suite executives

"When leadership is done right, it's both challenging and rewarding. You don't have to be on this journey alone! The ability to collaborate and build community will be one of the most coveted skills for future leaders in the coming decade. In *The Grassroots Leadership Revolution*, Glain Roberts-McCabe lays out the playbook for what you need to build your tribe to successfully navigate your career towards success. Packed with practical strategies, candour, and real-world examples, *The Grassroots Leadership Revolution* offers leaders a bullet-proof roadmap for success."

ANNA PETOSA, vice president, people operations, Pelmorex Corp. (The Weather Network)

"*The Grassroots Leadership Revolution* is the ultimate playbook for building a group coaching community that will support your leadership ambitions. This book is packed with practical advice, real-world stories, and easy-to-follow exercises, and is a terrific resource for leaders and group coaches alike. Glain Roberts-McCabe has taken abstract leadership ideas and made them pragmatic."

MARSHALL GOLDSMITH, *Thinkers 50* #1 Executive Coach for 10 years

"Glain Roberts-McCabe has opened up her treasure chest of resources and made them available for all. In doing so, she is equipping leaders with everything they need to successfully launch their own peer coaching community—the process, tools, and years of hard earned wisdom! *The Grassroots Leadership Revolution* is a must-have guide for any leader looking to grow their leadership capability—with and through others!"

JANEY PIROLI, vice president, global organizational development, McCain

"*The Grassroots Leadership Revolution* provides a step-by-step guide for creating a peer coaching group to support, challenge, and enable career-building leaders. Glain Roberts-McCabe shares her vast knowledge and in-depth experience in leadership development and coaching throughout the Recruit, Engage, Accelerate, and Perform sections. The practical and easy-to-use exercises and guides transform this excellent resource into a rock-solid action plan. I highly recommend this book to leaders at all levels who want to join forces with like-minded peers to achieve their purpose, follow their passion, and realize their ambitions."

PHIL BUCKLEY, author of *Change with Confidence*

"*The Grassroots Leadership Revolution* is a must-read primer for anyone who wants to grow the leadership mindset required to navigate unprecedented change and disruption. Read this book if you want to learn from one of the best. Start your own personal leadership revolution while building a trusted network using the power of your own peer coaching group."

DR. LAURA HAUSER, internationally recognized team coaching expert; creator of the Team Coaching Operating System™

"Whether you are a new or an experienced leader, your current and future success largely rests on your learning agility. And in today's fast-paced, networked and collaboration-centric organizations, you need others to accelerate your learning. You can't go it alone! In *The Grassroots Leadership Revolution* Glain Roberts-McCabe provides you with the practical roadmap for building a community to support your leadership to not only survive, but to thrive. Learn to leverage peer group coaching to avoid isolation, to foster innovation, to solve complex challenges, to reinvent yourself and more. A generous playbook chock full of game changing and fun leadership exercises and hacks. A must read for all leaders!"

KRISTER LOWE, PhD, Founder & CEO, Team Coaching Zone

"Glain Roberts-McCabe has delivered a unique, practical step-by-step guide for individuals and organizations that have a desire to improve themselves and perform at higher levels by becoming better listeners, coaches, networkers, and leaders!"

DAVE MONCUR, vice president, human resources, PepsiCo Foods Canada

"This is *the* book for those on a continuous journey to improve their leadership abilities. Glain Roberts-McCabe offers a simple and straightforward 'choose your own adventure' roadmap to create the right kind of coaching community for you and your peers."

LISA KIMMEL, ICD.D, chair & CEO, Edelman Canada; chair, Latin America and Global Women's Equality Network

The Grassroots Leadership Revolution

Build a Peer Coaching
Community and
Own Your Career

Glain Roberts-McCabe

THE ROUNDTABLE PRESS

Copyright © 2020 by Glain Roberts-McCabe

All rights reserved. No part of this book may be reproduced, stored in a retrieval system or transmitted, in any form or by any means, without the prior written consent of the publisher or a licence from The Canadian Copyright Licensing Agency (Access Copyright). For a copyright licence, visit www.access-copyright.ca or call toll free to 1-800-893-5777.

Cataloguing in publication information is available from Library and Archives Canada.
ISBN 978-1-9992436-0-9 (paperback)
ISBN 978-1-9992436-1-6 (ebook)

Some names and identifying details have been changed to protect the privacy of individuals.

Produced by
Page Two
www.pagetwo.com

Cover and Interior design by Setareh Ashrafologhalai
Interior photo courtesy of Carole B. Eves Photography
Interior illustrations by: Michelle Clement

THE ROUNDTABLE PRESS
www.goroundtable.com

*This book is dedicated to my daughter,
Nia Catherine McCabe. When she was five, and
I was scrolling through my Blackberry for the
thousandth time, Nia looked up at me with her big
blue eyes and asked, "Momma, do you love
me as much as you love your clients?" Thank you,
my darling child, for reminding me every day
what the real priorities in life are all about.
I love you to infinity and beyond.*

Contents

Introduction
Start Your Own
Grassroots Revolution

J IM IS THIRTY-FIVE and has been with his company for over ten years. He just missed out on his third promotion and is questioning whether he is ever going to get ahead.

Sayed is head of manufacturing at a global company and is continuously praised by his boss for delivering stellar results. Meanwhile, his new wife is ready to leave him because of the eighty-hour work weeks he is grinding out just to keep his head above water.

Annabel has been promoted to lead her department. All her former peers are now her direct reports and none of them seem all that thrilled that she was "the chosen one." She finds herself crying in the bathroom at least once a week and isn't exactly sure why.

Steven's wife just had a miscarriage (their third) and his boss let him know that he won't be getting the promotion and raise he'd been promised. Instead, he's being moved to lead a six-month project at their satellite location, which is a two-hour commute away from his home. He's worried about the impact the commute will have on his wife.

Louise's mom died unexpectedly. She took a week off but is back on the job to help pull her team through year-end budgeting. Everyone keeps telling her how amazing she is because she's still smiling and hasn't dropped any deliverables despite grieving her mom's death. Louise feels like a raw nerve that's covered with a thin veneer that could shatter at any moment.

As you read these real-life scenarios, my guess is that you can relate to several of them. Maybe you've even lived through them yourself, or something similar.

I'VE HEARD ALL of these stories—plus hundreds more—in the group coaching sessions we run at The Roundtable, an organization that helps leaders develop the strong coaching and collaboration skills necessary to navigate growth, disruption, and change. We hear from leaders who are facing challenges and pressures from both inside and outside of work. They feel like their job is to hold everything together, while at the same time they're barely holding on.

As leaders, we often look around and believe that everyone else has their shit together; that we're the only ones who are in over our heads. Nothing could be further from the truth.

I spent my twenties and thirties in management positions in the not-for-profit, public, and private sectors. I stumbled into leadership and, like many of us, enrolled in the school of "sink or swim," with a major in "initiation by fire." I spent many sleepless nights questioning if I was making the right career choices, and many more hours piling pressure on myself that left me feeling lonely and isolated.

In 2001, I found myself in the role of Managing Partner at a leadership consultancy that offered everything from executive coaching to traditional classroom-based training workshops. While managing the business, I also reveled in the opportunity to take as many leadership and management courses as I could. It was like drinking from a leadership firehose. I read hundreds of books and articles about leadership, attended conferences and workshops with top thought leaders like Stephen Covey, Ken Blanchard, John Maxwell, and others, and completed countless assessments that helped me deepen my self-insight.

Despite all of this access to structured professional development and leadership education, I began to realize that some of my greatest leadership insights were coming from interactions with like-minded colleagues, not from our classroom sessions.

With this in mind, I started to think about the team of consultants and coaches I led who were all leadership experts, and the many things I simply couldn't discuss with them. I recognized I needed a sounding board, and wanted to be able to tap into the wisdom of other leaders who could relate to the challenges I was facing. I wanted to connect directly with people who had faced similar leadership experiences.

I envied CEOs who had councils, advisory groups, peer groups, or Mastermind groups with whom they could connect and commiserate. At the time, these groups were only available to those holding the top jobs, not to leaders like me: ambitious mid-career types, with a hunger to keep learning and growing. I began to look for opportunities to connect with other leaders beyond the boundaries of our mid-sized consultancy. Where was my tribe?

In 2007, I decided to create the opportunity myself. I started The Roundtable with a vision of creating a place where smart, ambitious leaders could cultivate their leadership capabilities and capacity *together*. Our hallmark program is a peer-based group coaching program called The Roundtable for Leaders™. Small groups of leaders work together over an eleven-month period, meeting every six weeks to work on their leadership mindset and behaviours. The program is a combination of group coaching sessions, interesting leadership topics, peer accountability, online resources, and individual coaching sessions.

Our goal is to encourage self-exploration and autonomy, to troubleshoot real problems, and to develop the superior coaching skills leaders need to navigate ongoing change and disruption—all while building a trusted network. As our member Carla aptly said, we're "teaching leaders how to fish for themselves." In The Roundtable for Leaders program, participants learn lifelong skills that they can apply throughout their careers, but what everyone values most is the relationship they forge with a like-minded group of peers.

We've helped over-extended leaders learn to let go, newly promoted managers swim instead of sink, and leaders in transition find their footing. This was the case with Samantha, who embarked on The Roundtable for Leaders program with other members of her organization.

Samantha had returned from maternity leave and her entire world had turned upside down. Her allies had moved on, her boss was new to her, and a promotion that she had been promised had gone to someone else. Within fifteen minutes of our onboarding session, she was in tears. "I don't want to stay in this organization," she said, "I think I need to leave."

It's not the first time—and probably won't be the last time—that I've had to talk a smart, ambitious leader off the career ledge. Samantha, like many others I work with—probably like you reading this book—was smart, ambitious, driven and, at the time, also overwhelmed with change and struggling to navigate a shifting landscape with the mistaken belief that she had to do it all on her own.

"The best time is during the struggle. The top of the mountain is usually small, freezing, and lonesome. To this day I'm continually reinvesting myself in something new. I'm not afraid to start as a beginner in anything."

DAVID LEE ROTH
lead singer of Van Halen

Why We Need a Revolution

It's no secret that leadership can be lonely, not just "at the top," but at all stages of your career. There is increased pressure on leaders to do more with less, to be agile and adaptive to the shifting demands of business, and to balance driving results while caring about people. On top of everything, we *think* we know the plan, and then *bam!* Everything gets upended. We're drowning in unrelenting change and pressure.

This pace of change is too rapid to wait for HR departments to create a new learning program that will be outdated in twelve months. I believe it's time for leaders to take control of their own careers and not rely on their managers to set their course. It's time to break down the walls that we place around ourselves as leaders. It's time to shed the self-created armor that says, "I've got this all figured out. I'm in control, and I don't need your help."

It's time to stop trying to go at it alone.

It's time to start a grassroots leadership revolution by joining forces with other ambitious leaders. A community of like-minded peers will help you navigate the ups and downs of leadership and avoid the career pitfalls in a work world that refuses to slow down.

How to Use This Book

This book is the culmination of what I've learned over the past two decades of working with some of the best and brightest leaders in some of the world's greatest brands like PepsiCo, Walmart, CAA Club Group of Companies and the Toronto International Film Festival. I'm sharing the step-by-step process we use in our multi-award-winning Roundtable for Leaders group coaching program so you can create your own peer coaching group, and together successfully take command of your leadership career.

This book is divided into three key parts:

Part I gives you a playbook to **recruit** and **engage** your own leadership peer coaching group, as well as a formula for running peer coaching sessions successfully.

Part II, goes into detail on a core set of leadership topics that will **accelerate** your group members to strengthen their individual and collective leadership capacity.

In Part III, you'll learn how to keep your community energized, as well as some of the things to watch out for as you work together. We'll also explore how to bring many of the concepts back to your own teams so that you can build community and increase **performance** within your organization.

Design Your Journey

How you choose to run your group sessions is really up to you. You can be more structured in your approach, or a little looser. Here are three paths you can consider.

Choose your path	Chapters to Reference (in order)
The Loose Path: *I want to learn the basics of creating and running a peer coaching group. I'd like some flexibility with topics and want it to be more focused on exploring immediate issues with my peers.*	You can concentrate on Part II of the book and the activities in chapters 3, 4, 5, 6, and 13.
The Structured Path: *I really want to deep dive into my leadership development with others and would like some specific exercises to follow that we can all complete, and hold each other accountable to, together.*	Follow chapters 3, 4, 5 (optional), 7, 8, 9, 10, 11, 12, 13.
The Mixer: *I'd like to do some peer coaching and spontaneous discussions along with some more formal activities.*	If you'd like to mix it up a bit, then consider alternating a pure peer coaching session (see chapter 5) with some of the content chapters. For example: 3, 4, 5, 7, 5, 8, 5, 9, 5, etc. or add your own topics (see chapter 6 for ideas).

You may find it useful to provide copies of this book to your group members so that you can work through the materials together, but it isn't crucial. Throughout the book you will find a number of resources available on the Grassroots Leadership website (www.grassrootsleadershipbook.com) to help you run your group sessions. Watch for these symbols:

↓ Downloadable worksheets and handouts for your group.

📖 The playbook for your sessions.

☆ Chapter highlights with key tips and take-aways.

I'M SO GRATEFUL that you've picked up this book, and I'm excited to share our well-researched and proven approach with you. Becoming a great leader isn't a one-off training event, it's an ongoing journey. Consider *The Grassroots Leadership Revolution* your guide for creating a community of like-minded leaders who will support, challenge, and help you navigate today's disruptive world of work.

And, in case you're wondering what happened to Samantha, who I mentioned earlier, she's doing incredibly well. She leveraged her Roundtable experience to reset expectations with her new manager, and worked through her disappointment over not receiving a promotion with her peer group. She's still at the same company and thriving, with plenty of challenges and variety in her job. Samantha learned how to ask for what she wants and continues to grow as a leader, and as a mom. She continues to leverage the relationships she formed in her Roundtable peer coaching group as she navigates her next stage of career growth.

Before we jump into pulling together your group, I want to share why your ability to build and maintain community is going to be one of the most crucial skills for leaders. We're in the Age of Collaboration and your ability to grow and leverage networks is going to be one of your career gamechangers. Let's take a closer look.

It's Not You—Leadership Can Really Suck

A S AN EXECUTIVE coach I'm often asked, "What will trip up a leader's career?" There are probably a thousand different responses, but I find the answers fall into two areas: external factors and internal factors. There are many external factors that contribute to the complexity of leadership, and create unprecedented pressure on leaders—if you think it's harder to lead today than it was in decades gone by, you're not wrong. The fact that the term VUCA (volatile, uncertain, complex, and ambiguous) has made its way into the lexicon of corporate jargon speaks volumes to the challenges of leadership. After all, the US Army War College coined VUCA to describe conditions after the Cold War.

We've moved beyond the Age of Knowledge (marked by technology) to the Age of Collaboration (marked by networks and connection). This shift is demanding a change in how we lead—and how we grow as leaders. As Mila N. Baker asserts in her book *Peer-to-Peer Leadership*, "Leadership in today's world requires insight from more than one individual. We must rely constantly on others' insight, even when we are in positions of authority." Today we need *to rely on others* to get our work done. We leverage our networks to understand what data is vital to pay attention to and what isn't. We innovate through collaboration and diverse perspectives. We benefit from the camaraderie and relationships that we build through making connections and working together.

Bob Johansen, author of *The New Leadership Literacies* and distinguished fellow at the Institute for the Future in the Silicon Valley, describes the time we're in as a "scramble" with an explosion of connectivity and upheaval heading our way. It's a time that most leaders aren't ready for, Johansen asserts. Leadership in the future will be much less centralized and much more distributed. Having close relationships and looking for ways to grow collectively will be crucial skills for next-generation leaders. Networks will become a strategic priority for leaders seeking to navigate a world of relentless uncertainty and change; peer coaching groups will be a way to leverage the knowledge gained from such groups and accelerate it into action.

Let's take a closer look at three critical circumstances that both Baker and Johansen speak to, and the implications for leaders as we navigate our way through the "scramble."

1   There are more people involved in our work.

2   We are being bombarded with information and data.

3   Relentless disruption is forcing us to be agile and to innovate.

We'll also look at a fourth bonus external factor that I call "the manager effect."

1. There Are More People Involved in Our Work

Today, as we look across industries, we see fewer and fewer roles where individuals work on discrete parts of projects. Cost-cutting, downsizing, and the increasing influence of technology across divisions have increased the need to collaborate with other teams, coordinate efforts, and balance competing mandates to get the job done.

Decision-making through a hierarchy is becoming increasingly ineffective. Informal networks are proving to have more power to effect change—think the Arab Spring, or student Greta Thunberg's call to action on the climate crisis. And, as younger leaders enter the workplace, this networked approach to driving change, problem-solving, and communicating will shift how we lead and manage our organizations.

Up-and-coming organizations and industry disruptors are embracing nimbler organizational styles and horizontal leadership, but many traditional companies continue to cling to the hierarchical structures that they were founded upon. Instead of changing their outdated ways, companies continue to expect middle managers to be able to navigate successfully within them.

The implication for leaders is that we need to continuously cultivate our network and broaden our understanding of our organizations—both the internal and external forces and influences—in order to manage through the ambiguity that comes with disruption. Deep subject matter expertise becomes irrelevant without an understanding of how to integrate it across the organizational system. Informal influence, persuasion, and the ability to "connect the dots" between our area of the business and others are now essential skills.

The time of the "lone genius" or "arrogant expert" is fading quickly. As Netflix CEO Reid Hastings famously outlined in a 2009 PowerPoint deck on Netflix Culture: Freedom & Responsibility,

"Brilliant jerks. Some companies tolerate them. For us, cost to effective teamwork is too high."

Today's superstar leaders will be those who know how to artfully collaborate with colleagues in order to produce results. A diverse and well-connected peer group will provide you with knowledge and increased perspective, and will help you develop the crucial community-building skills required to lead in an increasingly interconnected workplace.

Key leadership implication: Collaboration will be the most prized capability of future leaders.

2. We Are Being Bombarded with Information and Data

With the rapid rise of technology and plethora of data and analytics available, it is simply impossible to stay ahead of all the information. Yet, organizations are looking for leaders who know how to prioritize the "big bets" and strategically make the right calls on new innovations.

It's often said that the further you go up the leadership ladder, the less you need to have the right answers, and the more you need to *ask the right questions*. With today's rapid change, you also need to know *where* to direct those questions. Which person in your strategic network has the insights and information you need? Do you know who can shortcut your learning to give you the facts or analyze the data to tell you what is important to pay attention to?

In Michael Watkins's excellent book *The First 90 Days*, he talks about the key things that leaders need to do to ramp up quickly and be successful as they take on a new role. One of the key activities in those crucial first ninety days is to take time to build alliances with those individuals who will be key to helping you succeed. Building these alliances needs to extend well beyond the first ninety days, or within the context of a new role. A strong, vibrant peer group will be critical to help you manage and navigate the increasing pace of information, and expand your understanding of who to go to for expert advice.

Key leadership implication: Knowing who to ask is as important as what to ask.

3. Relentless Disruption Is Forcing Us to Be Agile and to Innovate

The increasing speed of change is creating ambiguity across industries and causing a ripple of disruption that is hard to predict day to day, let alone on a five-year plan. It's also driving a requirement for leaders to be agile and innovate on a regular basis.

Innovation demands that we get out of our comfort zones and find new ways of looking at situations. Diversity of thinking brings the best ideas to the table, whereas groupthink will paralyze you.

Bob Johansen observes that "leaders will have to fail gracefully at the edge of their competence, without pretending that they know what they don't know." Connecting with others outside of your primary functional area, and even your organization, is a crucial tool for encouraging new ways of thinking and building mental agility. The challenge for most leaders is that we are so buried in the day-to-day pressures of the business that these kinds of exchanges aren't an immediate priority.

Peer groups offer a strategic support system to help you navigate beyond your comfort zone. They also provide you with a trusted support network when things don't go quite as planned.

Key leadership implication: Broadening your network both internally and externally will increase your learning agility and strengthen your innovation muscle.

Bonus: The Manager Effect

The relationship that you have with your manager is probably one of the most critical factors that will shape your career opportunities—or shortfalls. Time after time, "relationship with my manager" appears in the top five reasons for people leaving their organizations. Many of us rely heavily on our managers to help guide our careers, and this blind faith is a problem because most managers are lousy career coaches— including me and you. Here are a few examples of reasons why career coaching is tough for most of us.

Managers have an agenda: As a manager, you can't tell me that you're going to be thrilled if your top performer comes to you and says they're leaving their position at the organization in order to do something else. My bet is that your first reaction (even if it's fleeting) is going to be "oh, f*ck." Nobody wants to lose great talent, especially if you feel like you've invested a lot of resources in developing that person. When a good person quits, the default for most managers is to go into "sales" mode. We up the salary and / or perks and try to lobby the person to stay. It's difficult to be neutral when a big part of you is thinking about what the loss will mean to you and the rest of your team. You can't be a great coach when your underlying motivation is your own agenda. And, frankly, it's tough for any manager to find the right balance between what's best for the company and best for the individual.

Managers avoid discomfort: If you have someone on your team who is good at something that makes *your* life easier, my guess is that you're not going to spend too much time trying to figure out if they actually enjoy doing that activity. As long as they're delivering results, it's easy to ignore the subtle (or not so subtle) cues that may indicate they're getting bored or disengaged. After all, who wants to open that can of worms by having a career conversation? We put our heads in the sand when we see people may be disengaging because the thought of losing them gives us a sick feeling about the amount of work that will come our way.

Managers don't know how to coach: Most coaching programs for managers are simply too focused on rudimentary skills like asking good questions and active listening. These are only part of the puzzle. To be a successful coach, you also have to be able to listen without judgment *and* be truly focused on the person—and not their problem—in order to guide them to the best solution. The solution that's best for them, not for you as the manager.

I'm not saying that managers don't need to up their coaching skills—of course they do. Being an effective coach is a critical skillset. The point I want to reinforce here is that until all managers are selfless enough that they're able to support their employees' best interests, it's probably a good idea for you to have some other people in your career corner.

In addition to all of the external pressures facing leaders today, there are also some significant internal factors that affect our ability to successfully navigate the complexities of leadership. Next up I'm going to share some of the most common ways I've seen leaders self-sabotage as they try to grow their careers. Buckle up, you may be in for a bumpy ride.

How Leadership Careers Derail

HAVE WORKED WITH highly ambitious and successful leaders for many years, and I've seen far too many flame-outs of promising careers. Although some of the reasons are unique, four common themes come up repeatedly.

1 Lack of self-insight.

2 Overusing "winning" behaviours.

3 Not adapting to shifting expectations.

4 Going it alone.

1. Lack of Self-Insight

When you lack self-insight, you're at risk of finding yourself in a job that makes you miserable or—even worse—behaving in a way that makes others miserable. Self-insight allows you to proactively manage your blind spots, triggers, and biases. The more you understand your motivators and drivers, the more capable you are of driving your career in the right direction—and doing it in a way that inflicts minimal collateral damage on those around you.

Here's the tricky part though: having self-insight but not acting on it is what will cause your career to falter. I've met many people who profess to "know themselves" very well but do very little to change their approaches. Which leads me to my next point: your strengths are a liability.

2. Overusing "Winning" Behaviours

World-renowned business coach Marshall Goldsmith helped me realize that, past a certain point, it's our behaviours, not our knowledge and skills, that have the highest likelihood of derailing our careers—as well as our personal lives. His book, *What Got You Here Won't Get You There*, is a game-changer for any leader.

Once you achieve a certain level of leadership success, *what* you do simply becomes a table stake. *How* you do what you do is what gets talked about in performance reviews.

Don't believe me? I was once on an executive team where we spent *forty-five minutes* debating whether or not someone was ready to become a partner because of their facial expressions and hand gestures.

Your behaviour will be a career enabler or limiter. We all possess leadership approaches that have allowed us to be successful, but when we overuse them, they can become a liability. For example, one of my clients loves brainstorming, and she's fantastic at coming up with ideas really quickly. One of the downsides to this strength is that she can get bored easily and will prematurely start chasing the next shiny object (squirrel!!). This can lead to distraction, confusion, and be overwhelming for her team because they're never certain about the priorities.

In the world of recruiting, there is an expression: "What you know gets you hired, but what you do will get you fired." And sometimes, what you do is what was needed two years ago, but not today!

3. Not Adapting to Shifting Expectations

Leadership is situational. As leaders, we need to continuously assess our approach to make sure we're adapting to the environment and therefore the expectations that are constantly shifting around us. What worked at one point in our leadership career might not work in another.

Case in point: for five years one of our clients, the president of a global division, was hitting it out of the park at work—at least from the perspective of his boss, the CEO, who was a marketing / sales guy. When his boss was replaced by a new CEO with a finance background, he didn't like what he saw on the profit and loss statement. Our guy, who put a lot of energy into brand building and awareness (read: spending money on marketing), went from being the toast of the company to a performance improvement plan within six months when the bottom-line results showed no improvement. The change in focus and seeming loss of autonomy (his boss started micromanaging him around his spending habits) rocked his confidence and led to power struggles with the new CEO. Ultimately, the president was exited from the company.

If it's not a new boss, then it's a change in strategic direction, rapid promotion or increase in scope, a merger or an acquisition... so many situational factors can change the game. You're in danger of missing opportunities unless you continually reassess where you are, or you might even find that your career is sinking because what used to be required and revered has changed.

4. Going It Alone

In 2017, former US surgeon general Vivek Murthy wrote an article for the *Harvard Business Review* called "Work and the Loneliness Epidemic," and in it he states that we need to be concerned about social connection in our current world. "Loneliness is a growing health epidemic," he writes. "We live in the most technologically connected age in the history of civilization, yet rates of loneliness have doubled since the 1980s. Today, over 40% of adults in America report feeling lonely, and research suggests that the real number may well be higher. Additionally, the number of people who report having a close confidante in their lives has been declining over the past few decades. In the workplace, many employees—and half of CEOs—report feeling lonely in their roles."

Over the past decade, I've watched phenomenal leaders opt out, burn out, and check out because of the loneliness and isolation that they've felt in leadership roles. Connecting to a community of like-minded leaders can help you navigate the inevitable highs and lows of leadership. You'll learn how to put together a kick-ass group and also what you need to do to set a solid foundation for working together in chapter 3.

Community = Accountability

It's not just the mental health of leaders that makes cultivating a leadership community so critical. When it comes to accomplishing our goals, research shows that having accountability to others increases our chances of success. This is particularly true when we're working to develop a new habit or behaviour. According to research by Marshall Goldsmith, leaders who engaged in consistent periodic follow-ups on their behaviour goals with key stakeholders were perceived as more effective than those who did not follow-up and did not share their goals with others. By building a community to support you in your leadership development you will not only be combating the loneliness and isolation that comes with the territory of leadership, you'll also be increasing your odds of achieving your goals and making lasting change.

So, now that you're fully convinced that going it alone is career suicide (or at least convinced enough to read on), it's time to get started recruiting your group.

ONE
_____

Recruit

3

Assemble Your Community

ONE OF THE key elements of any successful group coaching experience is the chance to coach each other through challenges and opportunities. Often referred to as Mastermind groups, this notion of bringing like-minded people together stems from the work of Napoleon Hill, who shed light on the power of Mastermind groups with his bestselling book *Think and Grow Rich*. Since then, thousands of entrepreneurs and CEOs have tapped into the Mastermind concept to achieve higher degrees of success.

A Mastermind group is essentially a peer community that can function like your personal board of directors. It is a group of people who you respect, whose opinions you value, and who will ultimately share your enthusiasm for the process. At The Roundtable, we use elements of the Mastermind method in our approach that you will dive into in chapter 5. Before you start rounding people up for your group, let's slow it down and first look at the foundations for overall success.

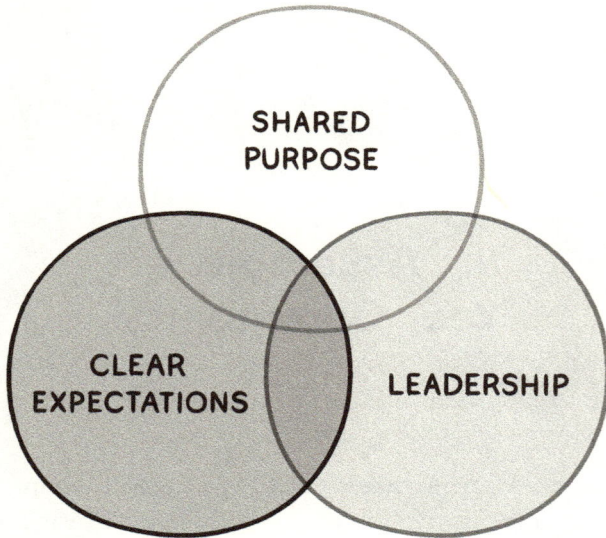

Shared Purpose

As you think of who you'd like to include in your group, consider people who have a shared interest in personal development, are willing to be open and share experiences, and are ready to make a commitment to the group. Ideally you will want to recruit members to your group who demonstrate partnership qualities, and avoid those who will be too high-maintenance and create headaches. This doesn't mean you should only recruit your friends or people that are like you. Be sure to go for diversity of thought as well as leadership style and approach.

The Importance of Commitment

Let's look at commitment more closely and how it affects the group experience.

- **Personal Commitment:** the degree to which an individual believes the group will help them advance their personal goals.

- **Group Commitment:** the degree to which an individual will set aside their personal goals to advance the collective goals in the group.

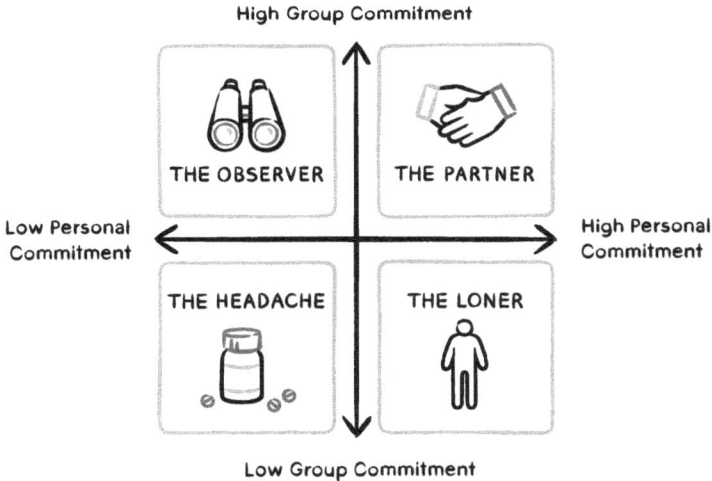

High Group Commitment

THE OBSERVER   THE PARTNER

Low Personal Commitment   High Personal Commitment

THE HEADACHE   THE LONER

Low Group Commitment

"You become like the five people you spend the most time with. Choose wisely."

JIM ROHN

American entrepreneur, author, and motivational speaker

The Loner = High Personal Commitment + Low Group Commitment

What it looks like: The Loner will consistently miss group sessions and commitments because they prioritize their personal commitments (e.g.: "I didn't look at the pre-read because I had to finish a project at work"). At the meetings, they tend to take up a lot of airtime talking about their issues and opportunities, but tune out when others' issues are put forward.

Why it happens: When the Loner is under pressure for performance targets, they'll find it easier to prioritize work goals over group sessions. Loners may not have a high motivation to belong to a group, and find limited value in putting their own needs aside to support others.

The Headache = Low Personal Commitment + Low Group Commitment

What it looks like: The Headache won't be committed to their own goals or the collective goals of the group. They don't do their "homework," they show up late (if at all), and are "in and out" of the group experience.

Why it happens: There simply isn't enough of a "what's in it for me?" for this individual. Perhaps they said yes because of FOMO (fear of missing out), or maybe they're too overcommitted and shouldn't have said yes in the first place.

The Observer = Low Personal Commitment + High Group Commitment

What it looks like: These individuals appear to support others in the group but aren't willing to share their own vulnerabilities. This behaviour can slow down trust within the group, and will eventually cause the Observer to become isolated.

Why it happens: There may be trust issues with individuals in the group that may need to be explored. In some cases, perhaps the Observer doesn't feel like they're a "good fit" for the group and / or needs some encouragement to go "all-in."

The Partner = High Personal Commitment + High Group Commitment

What it looks like: Magic happens when individuals within a group share and support each other, and are fully committed to the group purpose and objectives. Openness and vulnerability are high within groups as leaders learn *from* each other and *with* each other.

Why it happens: Individuals are personally motivated around their goals, and are equally motivated to make the group experience work. There is a feeling of shared success and camaraderie. At the core, this group is a high performing team.

Now it's time to decide who you might invite into your group. Grab a piece of paper and brainstorm who you can invite, what perspective you believe they'll bring to the group, and why they might be interested in joining. See our sample below.

Potential members	What they bring	Why they may be interested
Phil	Deep understanding of the organization.	Recently got promoted and was talking about needing a peer group.
Sayed	Marketing background. External perspective.	Joined 6 months ago and interested in meeting more peers.
Fawna	Worked in the field and recently joined head office.	Just returned from mat leave and interested in reconnecting with peers.

Clear Expectations

Without well-established "rules of the road," people will create their own. There are three areas to set expectations around: attendance, time commitment, and the responsibilities of participants.

1. Attendance

Making a commitment to attend the group sessions is crucial. Your group simply won't gain momentum if people show up late for the sessions or don't attend on a regular basis, so it's a good idea to draw some lines in the sand around what your expectations are for participation. Many of the CEO,

Mastermind, and peer groups have a "two strikes and you're out" clause (miss two meetings and you'll default your position in the group). Others have monetary fines. Whatever you decide to do, the key is to clearly define the expectations upfront so that people know what they're getting into.

What will the consequences be if people miss a session?

2. Time Commitment

CEO groups usually require a twelve-month commitment with monthly meetings. My suggestion is to start with a six- to eight-month commitment, with an option to extend by another six months. This allows the group enough time to get a feel for the process and assess its value, but doesn't feel too arduous.

If you decide to follow the framework laid out in this book, then your sessions will be ninety-minute to two-hour sessions every month (choose two hours if you have more than four people in your group).

Pro tip: Pick the same day of the month for your meetings (e.g., the third Thursday) to make it easier for people to remember and to stick with.

Next, pick a time of day that you know will work best for your group. Some people prefer early breakfast sessions. One of my friends has a group that meets for a ninety-minute Friday lunch once a month. Others do Saturday mornings. The key is to choose something that's going to be easy for everyone to manage. If members of your group have daycare drop-off or after-work activities, you'll need to factor it into your timing.

Finally, you need to decide if you want to meet virtually or in person. With platforms like Skype and Zoom, virtual sessions are highly manageable and probably the easiest to coordinate if you're assembling a group outside of your organization.

If you go with a virtual format, try your first meeting in person if you're able. It's a great way to accelerate the trust and camaraderie of the group, and will give you a solid foundation for the remaining sessions.

Plan Your Meeting Framework

Length of meeting

Frequency of meeting

Format of meeting (in person / virtual / both)

Summarize Your Group Expectations

Group members will need to commit to attending meetings on a _____ basis for _____ hours per meeting for _____ months. If a meeting is missed _____ times, the consequence will be _____.

3. Roles and Responsibilities of Participants

There are three roles that will help your group stay on track. One person could play all three, but I would recommend dividing them up to share the workload.

1. **Coordinator:** Sets up the agreed-to meeting schedule and sends out the reminders.

2. **Time Keeper:** Keeps things on track during each session.

3. **Facilitator:** Keeps the session on process. This role can be rotated within the group, or one person could be formally appointed as facilitator each time.

Leadership

There is a myth that most peer groups are self-directed. The reality is that for any group to become self-directed, it needs to start with good leadership. One of the things I know for sure about successful peer groups is that a lot of responsibility rests on the shoulders of you, the leader. Even self-directed groups require leadership until the rhythm takes hold.

When I was starting my own business, I put together a peer group of sales professionals and called the group the Business Advisory Referral Network (BARN). I hand-selected the group, organized the agendas, and sent out the reminders. I put together the framework and we met monthly. Once I lost interest, it fell apart. So if you're going to start a peer group, it's essential to recognize the time investment that will be required to get your new endeavour up and running.

Here's what you can expect:

- Designing your community: 1–2 hours.
- Recruiting your community: 3–4 hours.

- Communicating / coordinating logistics: 1–2 hours per month minimum.
- Preparing for your sessions: 1–2 hours per month.

As a leader, you'll find that your group will go through various stages of development. The next few pages outline what you can expect at each stage and the role you'll need to play to help the group navigate each one. Be sure to reference this as your group gains momentum.

Stages of Group Development

A universal truth about teams is that a foundation of trust is critical for success. It's no different in a peer coaching group. Like any community that brings together diverse personalities with diverse challenges, there are proactive strategies you can take as group leader to ensure smooth transitions between the stages your group will go through to stay productive. You will be pivotal in helping the group gain momentum. And, as an added bonus, you'll be able to practice flexing your team coaching muscle!

The commonly used model for group (and team) development is Bruce Tuckman's Forming, Storming, Norming, and Performing. Here's an overview of what you might experience as your group evolves.

Forming: Sessions 1 and 2

As your group is forming, your focus as their leader will be on helping the other members get to know each other: you may know everyone already, but they may not know each other equally well. Your objective is to help people open up and establish a positive and energetic environment. Here are some things you can do to facilitate that:

- Make sure everyone is prepared by sending out reading materials in advance.
- With the group's input, set any relevant ground rules in addition to the standard suggestions in this book. This way, your group feels a stronger sense of ownership.
- Do a check-in at the end of your first few sessions: "What should we stop / start / continue?"
- Build in some time for welcomes and small talk at each meeting.

Storming: Sessions 2 and 3

As your group members become more comfortable with each other, differences may become apparent. It's important at this stage to address any issues around punctuality, attendance, confidentiality, etc. Also, watch for any potential conflict between group members or varying levels of trust. Here are a few things you can do at this stage:

- Revisit the guidelines for keys to success that your group set in session one.

- Address any breaches of ground rules or abilities to fulfill commitments with individual members of the group.

- Plan a social activity to accelerate trust, like going for lunch or dinner together after your meeting. Breaking bread is always a great way to get to know each other.

- Make sure that the times / locations for the sessions still meet the needs of members' schedules and energy levels.

Norming: Session 4-ish (depending on how quickly your group moves through stages one to three)

Your peer group should start establishing real trust and cohesiveness around session three or four. At this stage, you'll probably start to see more equal participation among members, increased member engagement, and more socializing between group members. As a group leader you can:

- Look for opportunities to encourage equal participation from all members.

- Keep checking in at the end of the meetings to ensure things are on track (stop / start / continue).

Performing: Session 5 and beyond

The sweet spot for any great peer group is when members trust each other and there is a high degree of engagement, vulnerability, and transparency. At this stage, it's tempting to start moving away from your structure and process in the peer coaching area—but don't. Sticking to the structure outlined will ensure you continue to get maximum value from your time together.

By session 5, you could consider changing the venue or bringing in a guest speaker as a way to shift energy levels. Or you could start to rotate group leadership as a way to shift the focus from you as the "owner" of the group, to collective ownership by all members.

Inviting Your Group

On page 32, you brainstormed a list of potential group members. Now it's time to narrow down your list. Four to five people total is a good number because it's large enough to work as a group, but also small enough to give each other airtime. Plus, smaller groups are easier to coordinate schedules than larger ones.

Here are a few factors to help you finalize your list as you consider your recruits.

1 **Pick peers:** For a peer group to work well, the individuals need to be, well, *peers.* You want people who can contribute to your learning as much as you can contribute to theirs. For the purpose of a leadership development experience it's helpful to be at a similar career stage. For example, a vice-president in their thirties may have different career and leadership ambitions than a vice-president from the same organization with one year left to retirement.

2 **Consider commitment and interest:** Not everyone is coachable. This is as true for one-to-one coaching as it is for building a peer coaching group. Not everyone is interested in developing themselves, and one of the biggest death knells to the group coaching experience is people who don't want to be there. Their energy will drain the group. In contrast, when you have a group of like-minded achievers, they tend to raise the bar on each other. I like to call this the positive side of peer pressure. Mutual respect is important at the table, so don't bring on people who don't meet your "partner" criteria.

3   **Look for cross-functionality and internal / external perspectives:** One of the greatest benefits of forming a peer coaching group is the ability to tap into a broad range of perspectives. After all, we want to build our agility muscle by exposing ourselves to a variety of views. Internal peer groups will help broaden your understanding of the organization, whereas external groups will provide you with a network of contacts and broader ideas. Decide if you want one or the other, or perhaps a mix of both. If you're inviting people from your office, create a cross-functional group (peers from different departments within the same organization) instead of choosing peers from the same team or area. This eliminates the natural competition and awkwardness that can sometimes arise when people work closely together; if they're in line for the same promotion or report to the same manager, for example. The benefit of having a peer group is the opportunity to explore ideas that you may not be able to explore within your team, so diversity in your group is a key element to foster successful conversations.

4   **Evaluate chemistry:** Make sure the people who you're inviting are those you enjoy and want to spend time with. The last thing you want to do in a peer group is find yourself becoming a referee having to manage difficult personalities. That being said, it bears repeating that you do want to look for diversity of thinking and approaches. You want people who will challenge you to grow outside of your comfort zone.

With your plan in place, start inviting your potential members to learn more about your vision. I find that sending a short email—maybe with an attached one-pager outlining the

The benefit of having a peer group is the opportunity to explore ideas that you may not be able to explore within your team.

purpose, format, and commitments—is a great place to start. It could look something like this:

Hi [name],

I'd like to invite you to join my peer coaching group at XYZ Company Breakfast Warriors. The plan is for five of us to meet monthly and follow the structure provided by *The Grassroots Leadership Revolution*. Together, we'll be exploring some critical topics that will help us support each other in upping our leadership game this year.

- Identifying our personal core values.
- Determining our individual zones of genius, and how to leverage more of these strengths at work.
- Building our personal brand.
- Developing goals.
- Plus other topics that we want to explore as a group.

Below is an outline of the purpose of the group, commitment required, and tentative schedule. I'm really excited about this opportunity, and hope you'll join me for coffee on [date] to learn more about the plan and confirm your participation.

[signature]
XYZ Company Breakfast Warriors

Purpose: To develop our leadership capability and exchange best practices using *The Grassroots Leadership Revolution*

Required commitment: Monthly breakfast meetings (90 minutes)

When and where: 3rd Thursday of every month, 7:30 a.m. to 9 a.m., breakfast place across from office

Introductory meeting: November 21 in the team meeting room from 12 to 1

Once you've invited your group, it's time for your introductory meeting. Here's how to do it right.

Introductory Meeting

The Introductory meeting is just that: a chance for you to describe your vision for the group, outline the format and the commitments, and determine if everyone is interested in participating. This meeting provides you with the opportunity to share your vision and the basic group ground rules and expectations in order to give people the opportunity to decide if it's right for them. If you've already spoken to everyone individually, then skip this meeting and head right into your first session. If not, here are a few things to discuss:

- Your vision for the group and its purpose.
- Why you selected the people in the room to participate.
- Time commitment and expectations.
- Overview of first meeting agenda (see chapter 4 for sample).
- Pre-work requirements for the sessions.

With your group members on board, it's time to set the date for the first session and provide any pre-session materials (outlined in chapter 4 and in the reference section beginning on page 153).

☆ CHAPTER 3 HIGHLIGHTS

- Clarify the purpose of your group before recruiting members.

- Outline the logistics and expectations of the commitment for group members.

- Consider the members of your group carefully, and hold an informal introductory session to confirm everyone's interest before diving into your first real session.

↓ Downloads Available for Chapter 3
- Tips on running virtual groups

Session 1
Accelerate Group Trust

O NCE YOUR GROUP members have given you a solid "I'm in!" then it's time for your first official group session. The objective here is to build trust within your group. Your goal is to create a safe space where members are willing to be vulnerable with each other. After all, the power of the peer group is your ability to help each other develop, and to support each other as leaders, and you'll never get there if you're not willing to open up and share.

The "V" Word

Let's talk a little bit about vulnerability. By definition it means to be susceptible to emotional injury—ouch! Leaders are typically not encouraged to be vulnerable; I know the word makes me a little squirmy, and don't even get me started on "intimacy!"

Leaders are told that we need to be brave and act courageously. We're told "never let them see you sweat." And yet, when it comes to creating a powerful leadership community that's there to support you, you need to do just that. It's the willingness to be vulnerable—to share what doesn't work, to list our foibles and failures—that allows others to open up, and for each of you to learn from each other.

Consider this: when have you learned the most in your life? From your successes or from your failures? By opening up and sharing all of our leadership "dirty laundry," we learn and grow together. This allows us to avoid pitfalls and accelerate our careers by gaining new insights, techniques, and tools that we can put into action straight away.

In her book *Dare to Lead*, author Brené Brown shares her theory that the foundational skill of courageous leadership is the willingness and ability to "rumble with vulnerability." In your own peer coaching group, you'll be creating a safe space where your peers can practice vulnerability and support each other in the "rumble."

To prime the pump for vulnerability, you need a foundation of trust. Here's a simple formula to get you started.

Confidentiality + Personal Sharing = Foundation of Trust

Your group offers members a unique opportunity to discuss sensitive issues in a safe environment. As such, it is imperative that members commit to keeping all items that are discussed during these sessions in the strictest confidence. One of the ways to ensure that groups are going to feel confident that "what's said in the room, stays in the room," is to have each person sign a confidentiality agreement at the start of the program. This simple act sends a strong message to the group about how seriously confidentiality is taken.

Once the expectation around confidentiality has been established, it's time to help the group build rapport.

Remember, the great advantage of peer groups is the opportunity to share real-life challenges and concerns, and to get support and feedback. However, sharing personal challenges may make people feel vulnerable. To build a foundation where group members can feel comfortable being candid, the first step is to deepen relationships and create what's known as "psychological safety": the belief that we can take interpersonal risks within a group and won't be ridiculed.

Getting to Know You:
Why It's Important to "Get Personal"

Work today has become hugely transactional, and—as we talked about in our opening chapters—people are feeling more and more socially isolated. We know each other by titles and job duties, not as people. One of the things that you need to do when forming your group is to establish a high level of openness and candour. You can accelerate this by helping people connect on a personal level.

There are lots of ways to make this happen, but here are my top three.

- **Personal collage:** Participants create a visual collage to share aspects of their lives including hobbies, values, things they're proud of, people who are important to them, etc. Artistic talent doesn't matter. Some people do full posterboard collages, others have done PowerPoint decks or Pinterest boards.

- **Object of significance:** In this exercise, participants bring in an object of significance from home. They share a story about its meaning and the impact it's had on them. I've seen everything from a grandmother's quilt, to a family picture taken in a special place, to a set of measuring scales.

- **Lifeline:** In this activity, participants create a "lifeline" based on high and low points they've experienced throughout their lives. It's fascinating to see what people include for the "life was great" versus "life was hard" sections.

Getting to know each other—as people not titles—is fundamental to accelerating trust and vulnerability. Yes, you will have people who express more about themselves than others. That's OK. I've found there's always someone in the group who's brave enough to share at a deeper level. Invariably others will comment on that person as being the one who set the tone for the group. As group leader, you can role model vulnerability by going first and ensuring the right tone is set.

When you're wrapping up your first session, you can determine the group logistics, assign roles, and then finalize your schedule.

📖 Session 1 Playbook

Here's a basic agenda for your first session.

Session Length, 75–90 minutes

Timing	Activity
10 minutes, Welcome	• Leader welcomes group and shares vision / purpose. • Group members briefly introduce themselves.
5 minutes, Overview Expectations	• Discuss expectations around confidentiality and commitment. • Circulate confidentiality agreement.
45-60 minutes, Introductions	• Individual introductions (10 minutes per person), select one of the "getting to know you" exercises suggested in this chapter. • Encourage group members to ask questions to learn more about the individual. • Debrief the exercise by exploring the common areas within the group. How has this exercise shifted the energy in the group? Was anyone skeptical about doing this at first? How have your feelings changed (if at all)? How might we use an exercise like this with our teams?
5 minutes, Next Meeting	• Confirm next meeting location, timing, and details. • Discuss any pre-reading that may be required.

☆ CHAPTER 4 HIGHLIGHTS

- Vulnerability is the key to building trust and psychological safety within your group.

- Slowing down and getting to know each other provides an opportunity to build trust and camaraderie.

- Confidentiality agreements within the group set a clear intention and expectation for future sessions, allowing for a faster foundation of trust to develop.

↓ Downloads Available for Chapter 4
- Confidentiality agreement
- "Getting to know you" exercises and debrief tips
- Session agenda

TWO

Engage

5

Session 2
Peer Coaching 101

ONE OF THE greatest things about being part of a peer group is the opportunity to support and coach each other through immediate, real-life challenges and opportunities versus the typical leadership training programs that focus on academic and theoretical case studies. In addition, the coaching process creates a structure for accountability that helps group members achieve goals.

A Guide to Coaching Peers

When a group of smart leaders gets together to discuss a challenge, it's easy for individual opinions, personal biases, and agendas to get in the way of the actual issue. Smart people like to solve problems. Unfortunately, solving problems for another person is the opposite of what good coaching is all about.

In The Roundtable approach, we like to leverage both coaching skills and mentoring insights to help leaders progress. Before we look at our framework, let's take a quick look at coaching versus mentoring.

Coaching versus Mentoring

Coaching is a principle skill for any leader today, and being part of a peer group is an excellent way to continuously build your coaching muscle. It's also a great way to get mentoring on issues and opportunities that you're facing by tapping into the wisdom of the people in your group. Many people ask me, what is the difference between coaching and mentoring? Here's how we break it down:

Coaching

- Guided by the needs of the person being coached.
- Enables the coachee to find their own answers, with help from the coach.
- Focuses on improving immediate performance on the job.

Mentoring

- Guided by the goals of the person being mentored.
- Leverages the knowledge, experience, and expertise of the mentor.
- Addresses a longer-term vision and may not be job-focused (i.e., preparing you for the future by building broader leadership skills versus how to complete a task in your current role).

So, with these two elements in mind, let's look at what can happen when a group gets together to coach each other. Here's a typical scenario that I've seen play out many times:

Linda is struggling with her boss, who's an extreme micromanager. She can't seem to ever provide her with enough detail on anything. In their most recent team meeting, her boss called her out for not being able to answer questions that were the responsibility of one of her direct reports. Linda wants to talk to her boss about that incident but doesn't know how to approach the conversation.

She presents the issue to her peer group, and immediately heads start nodding in sympathy. Joe suggests that she talk to her boss about her expectations on levels of detail. Linda explains that she's already tried that once. Susan suggests that Linda share her concerns with HR. She goes on to explain that she had a similar experience and ultimately was able to move to another department. Joe and Alan start talking to Susan about what she did and how she did it.

Linda sits quietly as the others talk about this idea some more. They all seem to think this is the best course of action. Unfortunately for Linda, she doesn't actually want to move to another department, or complain to HR.

Would you say Linda got what she needed from her peer coaching experience? Probably not.

Without a clear process for coaching each other, group sessions can become free-for-alls, and a missed opportunity to help the individual who is being coached to make any progress.

Having a clear process that every member can follow to help coach each other through issues may feel laborious, but will get you to a better outcome. On the next page is a high level view of The Roundtable Peer Coaching Method™. We'll break down the key skills you'll need to successfully run a peer coaching group and then dive into the details of each element of the Method later in the chapter.

The Roundtable Peer Coaching Method

STEP 1: Headline
STEP 2: Select
STEP 3: Share
STEP 4: Coach
STEP 5: Confirm
STEP 6: Mentor
STEP 7: Reflect

In The Roundtable program, we balance both coaching and mentoring to help leaders move ahead. Here's how we visually describe the components of the skills required to effectively peer coach:

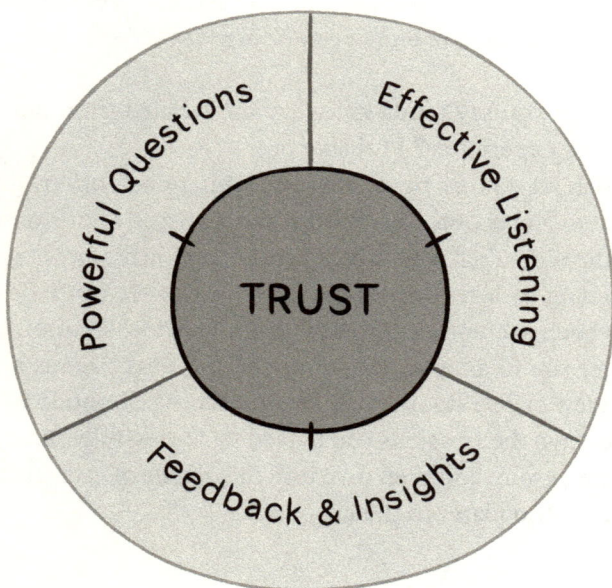

Powerful Questions and Effective Listening

At the first session, you started building a strong foundation of trust by taking the time to get to know each other personally, and by signing a group confidentiality agreement. This will provide a platform for the psychological safety needed to coach each other on real-time issues. It's important to continue to revisit the confidentiality agreement for your group as you go forward and / or introduce new members.

The next two essential skills for a strong peer coaching experience are asking powerful questions, and listening effectively. Let's take a closer look at each one.

Powerful Questions

Powerful questioning techniques will bring so much more information to the surface, and allow the group members to look at a situation or perspective from several different angles. This often leads to personal "aha" moments and learning opportunities. Here are some points to keep in mind to strengthen your "powerful questioning" ability.

- Avoid leading questions. (e.g., Have you tried...?)

- Explore feelings that relate to the situation. (e.g., What is holding you back? What's your biggest fear?)

- Ask contextual questions, but focus on questions that coach the "person," not the "problem." (e.g., What outcome do you want? What do you think your next step should be? What have you tried?)

- Keep your questions short and punchy. (e.g., What's the worst thing that can happen? What's your dream scenario here?)

Effective Listening

A good peer coach listens more than they talk. Here are a few tips to improve your listening skills.

- Listen for any unvoiced emotions, such as pauses in the conversation, energy, tone of voice.

- Observe clues from body language like eye contact, fidgeting, open or closed posture.

- Listen for assumptions, and language like "should," "must," or "have to."

- Pay attention to tone, body language, pauses etc. that may be in conflict with what's being said.

- Avoid making assumptions and get curious—don't take things at face value, dig deeper.

- Minimize distractions and pay attention.

- Make good eye contact.

- Jot down key points and phrases that the other person uses.

With our basic coaching skills covered, let's look at the mentoring component, which is providing feedback and insights. Mentoring allows members of the group to offer insights and feedback so that the individual can gain new perspectives on their situation, and build out their action plan.

Guidelines for Providing Feedback and Insights

Your peer is not your "direct report," so it's not your job to wag your finger and tell them what they "should" be doing in a specific situation. Instead, you have an opportunity to offer feedback and insights that will help them consider different actions and potential approaches to the situation.

When providing feedback and insights, there are a few great ways you can add value to your colleague without directing them on what to do:

- **Share experiences and lessons learned:** When you share stories of similar experiences that you've encountered and the lessons you've learned along the way, you're giving your colleague the opportunity to hear about some concrete, actionable activities that worked for you. It's up to them to take what they will from your stories and experiences. It doesn't mean that they need to take the same approach you did—think of it more as an opportunity for you to provide "lessons learned" as a way to short-cut their own learning.

- **Offer observational feedback:** Sometimes when a colleague is struggling, they need to be reminded of their strengths and / or capacity to overcome the challenge. Providing observational feedback is a good way to remind them of their capabilities. (E.g., "What I know about you is that you're really good at dealing with difficult situations and have all the skills you need to manage this tough conversation.")

- **Encourage them:** If your peer is wrestling with a highly sensitive or emotionally charged issue, sometimes the feedback they need is that you recognize the struggle and you support them. Offering words of encouragement is sometimes more important than sharing strategies. (E.g., "I can see that this is a really hard issue for you. You've got this and I'm here to help if you need to vent or talk some more about it.")

- **Share resources:** Perhaps you've read a book or know of someone who could be a good resource for the situation. Sharing knowledge is a great way to support peers in the peer coaching process.

Word of Warning: Focus on the Person, Not the Problem

Decision-making and problem-solving are two key qualities that are essential to successful leadership. It's likely been a factor in your previous promotions. Sadly, they are the skills that perpetually get in the way when leaders are coaching others.

But isn't solving the problem the ultimate goal of coaching?

Yes, *but* it's up to the person being coached to solve the problem—not the coach. Coaching philosophy suggests that the solutions, and the ideas for how to tackle the issue, are within the person being coached—they just need a little help and support to uncover these insights.

As a coach, your job is to help your peer gain the additional perspective needed to get to the heart of the matter, and find new potential solutions for the problems they are struggling to solve. Your job is not to do all the heavy lifting and problem-solving for them. Rather, it's to support, encourage, and deepen understanding, and to hold each other accountable to achieving what you said you were going to do.

Pulling It All Together

Here's how The Roundtable Peer Coaching Method looks step-by-step:

1 **Headline:** Group members share specific challenges / opportunities that they would like to bring up to the group in one or two sentences. The main objective here is to get all of the issues out on the table as quickly as possible. For example, "I'm having a problem with my manager who is being unclear on expectations." No other details are needed at this stage.

2 **Select:** Members prioritize the challenges / opportunities and select one to begin with. You can ask group members to share the urgency of their issue / opportunity, and look for people who may not have had the opportunity to receive peer coaching at prior sessions.

3 **Share:** The selected member can then share his / her challenge or opportunity in more detail. Give them five minutes to share the key elements of the situation. What have they tried, what's worked, etc.?

4 **Coach:** Group members then ask coaching questions (no advice or suggestions) to uncover root issues. During the coaching process, encourage your group to focus on the person being coached, not the problem they're trying to solve.

5 **Confirm:** Once you feel like enough questions have been asked (this is more art than science), it's time to shift to providing mentorship. Confirm with the member on the coaching seat where they would specifically like support.

6 **Mentor:** Members can then share experiences, observations, and insights to provide support, but don't give prescriptive recommendations or advice. By sticking with simple observations, encouragement, or shared experience, you are giving your colleague the opportunity to chart their own path and decide which course of action is best for them.

7 **Reflect:** The member being coached can now share their feedback and reactions to the experience, but not on the individual feedback given. Commenting on the value of each person's feedback is an evaluation and has the potential to shut people down. It's not about whose idea is "best," it's about getting the ideas out there.

It will be tempting—especially as your group gets comfortable with each other—to deviate from the process, but I encourage you to stick with it at least 80% of the time to really drive high-value outcomes. The facilitator for each session can be in charge of keeping the group on task.

"Lack of direction, not lack of time is " the problem."

ZIG ZIGLAR

author and
motivational speaker

A Closer Look at Accountability

One of the most powerful things a group experience can offer is peer accountability. Think about why exercise programs that involve other people (e.g., joining a running club and training for a marathon) or weight-loss programs that involve peer support groups as well as accountability check-ins are so successful. When you're trying to create new habits and shift behaviour, doing it together is easier than doing it alone.

The same holds true for your peer coaching group. Here are two ideas for upping accountability:

1. Setting Intentions

At the end of every session, ask group members to write down one or two intentions or commitments that they will stick with between now and whenever the group plans to meet again. Doing so will increase the likelihood of success. Dr. Gail Matthews, a psychology professor at the Dominican University in California, recently studied the art and science of goal setting and found that you become 42% more likely to achieve your goals and dreams simply by writing them down on a regular basis. Matthews also found that those who shared their goals with a friend were 70% more likely to attain said goals. The key is that you're sharing the goal with someone you trust. (Good thing you have a peer group, right?)

2. Progress Reporting

One of the greatest things we undervalue is the power of reflection. In our society, rushing from activity to activity and wearing the "badge of busy" is somehow equated with success. This constant running gives us very little time to reflect and integrate learning.

With this in mind, there is great value in pausing at the start of each of your sessions to check in and see what progress has been made. There are three questions to ask your group members:

1. What progress are you most proud of?
2. What have you learned from your actions?
3. What's your next priority / focus?

You can download and print our template to share with group members, or simply have everyone bring a journal with them to track their progress.

As a group, you may decide that you want to adopt the peer coaching structure as part of each meeting. You can typically do two to three rounds of peer coaching in sixty to ninety minutes.

📖 Session Two Playbook

Session Length, 80–95 minutes

Timing	Activity
5 minutes	• Leader welcomes group.
10 minutes	• Group provides updates on one success and one learning since the last meeting.
45 to 60 minutes, Peer Coaching	• Select 2 to 3 challenges based on time available.
10 minutes, Session Debrief	• What worked in our peer coaching session? • What coaching skills would you like to work on for next time? • How might you use this coaching structure with your teams?

| 10 minutes, Wrap Up | • Discuss next session pre-work (see Reader's Choice below). |
| | • Each person share one key commitment to be completed by next session. |

Reader's Choice

At the beginning of the book, I outlined three paths you could take with your peer groups:

- The Loose Path
- The Structured Path
- The Mixer

If you've chosen **The Loose Path**, you can now use the peer coaching process outlined in this chapter each time you come together. As you progress as a group, you can tap into some of the suggestions I've outlined in chapter 6 to keep your sessions vibrant.

If you've chosen **The Structured Path**, jump to Part 2 where I've outlined some session-by-session activities your group can do together. Note: the activities are designed to build off each other, but you can choose to do the ones that interest you the most.

If you chose **The Mixer**, then you can mix and match between the structured activities in Part 2 and the peer coaching structure outlined in this chapter. The choice is yours. My advice is to choose one approach and try it for at least three sessions before deciding to change.

☆ CHAPTER 5 HIGHLIGHTS

- Peer groups offer a unique opportunity to provide both coaching and mentoring support.

- As coaches, it's important to focus on the person, not the problem, by using core coaching skills of listening and asking powerful questions.

- Peer groups create the accountability support needed to keep group members on track—the positive side of peer pressure!

↓ Downloads Available for Chapter 5
- Powerful peer coaching questions
- Peer coach facilitator play-by-play
- Accountability template
- Session agenda

6

The Loose Path
Extra Resources

I F YOUR GROUP has decided to use The Loose Path rather
than following the session-by-session approach, this
chapter will give you some ideas on how to keep things
fresh and relevant. Some groups find great value in
keeping things simple and sticking to The Roundtable Peer
Coaching Method, whereas others enjoy digging into more
leadership topics. Let's look at some ways you can easily inject
some learning into your group gatherings.

Peer Learning

1. Make a list of leadership topics that interest your group.
   Find a TED Talk that features the topic, watch it before
   the session, and then get together and share your thoughts.
   TED even provides debrief questions that you can use.

2. Choose a leadership book and read it. Debrief it as a group. I've included some of our favourite leadership reads in the Resources section.

3. Select an article from the *Harvard Business Review* or similar publication, read it and discuss it.

4. Attend a conference together and exchange your key learnings.

5. Take turns presenting something you've recently learned about to your group. We learn by teaching, so teach your peers what you know.

6. Use a simple format called "needs and leads." Group members open each session sharing a new learning they've had, and then share a need they would like some group advice on that doesn't require coaching (e.g., I'm looking for a new ad agency, place to hold an offsite, speaker for a conference, etc.).

Deepen Relationships

For peer groups that have worked together for some time, digging deeper into getting to know each other is an excellent way to enrich the coaching experience.

Consider completing one of the "getting to know you" exercises outlined below, and take a session to explore the group members' answers in order to deepen relationships and enrich your conversations.

1) Complete a Free Online Assessment and Share Results

Possible discussion questions

- What are your strengths?

- What are the developmental areas you've decided to focus on?

- Why did you choose that area? How do you think it will help you in your leadership?

2) Refresh Your Career Visions

Explore

- How has your vision changed / evolved?

- How can your group support you in achieving your goals? (E.g., if you want to be healthier and have committed to going to the gym, will reviewing your progress with your group be helpful?)

3) Write Your Obituaries

Things to ask

- What do you want to be remembered for? How would you want to be described by friends, family, and coworkers?

- What habits, goals, and behaviours can you do today to move closer to your vision?

- How has your vision changed / evolved?

4) Goal Reviews

Discuss

- Share your goal progress with your group. If you're getting stuck / not moving forward on a goal, explore what is holding you back.

- Use your meetings as a way to stay on track and hold yourself accountable.

📖 General Session Playbook

Session Length, 70–90 minutes

Timing	Activity
5 minutes	• Leader welcomes group.
10 minutes	• Group provides updates on one success and one learning since the last meeting.
40 to 60 minutes	• Peer Learning session or Peer Coaching session (two issues).
10 minutes, Reflection	• What "aha" moments have you gained from this session? • What worked well with the group coaching? • What could you do better / differently next time?
5 minutes, Wrap Up	• Discuss next session pre-work (group decides). • Each person shares one key commitment to be completed by next session.

Tap Your Community

Remember, one of the greatest things about peer groups is the opportunity to build and extend your network.

My friend Charles Brown, President and CEO of LifeLabs, once told a group of Roundtable members that when it came to networking, it was more important to have twenty people who really have your back than 1200 contacts on LinkedIn. I couldn't agree more. By creating a community, you are automatically creating a powerhouse network.

Don't miss the opportunity to tap into the extended network that these relationships provide. Use your group to ask for referrals, job leads, mentors, or sponsors. By working together, you will build your social agility and deepen relationships with people who can help you advance your career goals.

☆ CHAPTER 6 HIGHLIGHTS

- Injecting new learning topics into your peer coaching groups will keep things "fresh."

- Taking time to get to know each other at a deeper level will enrich the group discussions.

- Seek ways to leverage your collective networks to strengthen your careers.

↓ Downloads Available for Chapter 6
- Accountability template
- Session agenda

THREE

Accelerate

7

Grow Your Leadership Impact
The Structured Path

F YOUR GROUP is interested in following The Structured Path and diving into some very specific leadership topics and setting some concrete goals for your leadership careers, then this section is for you. In it, you'll find a series of activities that you can do to strengthen your leadership capability both individually and collectively. You and your group members can revisit these exercises as your careers evolve.

Earlier, we explored ways that we can unintentionally derail our leadership career paths. In this section, we're going to look at some of the foundational pieces of great leadership so that you and your group keep things headed in the right directions.

There are thousands of leadership models out there. Your organization likely has one of its own. Maybe they've had several over the years!

After reviewing hundreds of different leadership theories, books, and competency models, here's what I've observed: when it comes to leadership, we need to be intentional. At

its core, leadership begins with self-insight. From there—as leaders—we help people grow, deliver results, and do it all with purpose. After all, it's hard to inspire followership if you can't connect to a higher purpose beyond pushing paper or producing widgets.

Self-Insight

We develop self-insight by becoming aware of our actions, gaining a deeper understanding of the impact of our approach, and aligning these insights with our own ambitions. In my experience, it's a never-ending process. You won't simply wake up one day and say, "I completely know myself and am now the perfect leader." (Although I know we've all encountered people who would probably disagree with that remark and insist that they've got things all figured out!) As humans, we are constantly evolving, and new situations and experiences awaken deeper layers within ourselves. You can't put "develop self-insight" on a checklist and mark it as complete, "one and done." Keep "progress not perfection" as your mantra for evolving as a leader.

As we cultivate our self-insight, we are able to bring more intentionality to our leadership approach. Intentional leadership means showing up, having a plan, being mindful of our actions and impacts, and setting a clear direction for ourselves first and foremost. With self-insight as a foundation, the rest of our career decisions become much easier to navigate.

"If you don't know where you're going, any road will get you there."

GEORGE HARRISON

Richard's Story

Richard was the head of strategy for a fast-growing digital organization. He was well-liked at work, enjoyed his colleagues, and appreciated the perks (including being able to bring his dog into the office), but ultimately wasn't feeling fully engaged.

As Rich worked through elements of The Roundtable for Leaders program with his peers, it became increasingly clear to him—and to those in the group—that his personal ambitions were out of alignment with his role. Session after session, while others in the group were making progress, Rich was feeling stuck. He simply couldn't seem to get enthusiastic about any of the goals he was setting.

During a one-to-one coaching session I asked him, "If you could do anything, what would you do?"

Banging his hands on the table, he exclaimed, "I'd be a film director!" He arrived at the next group session with an energy and passion we hadn't seen before. He was able to leverage the peer session to explore the idea more fully and come up with a plan to have a conversation with his boss.

This clarity provided Richard with a clear direction. Within months he had left his job and fully shifted his career path. When you're that far out of alignment with your own ambitions, it doesn't really matter how great your workplace is; getting clear on where your passions lie allows you to work in partnership with your employer.

After they'd had a candid conversation, Rich's manager didn't have to waste unnecessary time trying to convince him to stay. This wasn't about providing Rich with a new role or a new perk. Any of those things would have been short-term solutions. Rich had found his passion. As a manager, you can't argue with that.

Many of us are like Rich and trip into leadership roles by accident. We're good at what we were hired to do, and then we find ourselves being promoted to lead others. In the early stages of our careers we can fixate on the next rung in the ladder and lose sight of the longer career path that we want to be on. As the expression goes, there's nothing worse than climbing the ladder and then finding that you've placed it on the wrong wall.

Awareness, Ambitions, Approach

Getting clear on your own ambitions is a critical first step in any leadership journey. One of the exercises you will do with your group will be to explore your values (chapter 8), your strengths (chapter 9), and use those insights to create a three-year career vision. Your career vision will be your "true north" as you navigate the options and opportunities that may come your way. Without a career vision, it's easy to feel the pressure to say "yes" to opportunities that ultimately don't satisfy us. With a career vision, we can be clearer and more articulate with our managers about the opportunities and experiences we would like to have.

We'll also begin to examine the approach you're taking to your leadership. What behaviours will support you in achieving that vision, and what will hold you back? What is your personal brand? We'll address each of these questions and steps in chapters 10 and 11.

Finally, with this deeper awareness of who you are and where you'd like to take your career, you will be able to develop a clear plan forward and, with the support of your peer community, will have the support, encouragement, and accountability to implement that plan successfully.

Let's start by looking at our values, which provide a baseline for career—and life—satisfaction.

8

Determine
Your Values

ONE OF THE core elements of self-insight is understanding our values. Our values are like a personal compass that help us make decisions, fuel our job satisfaction and engagement, and create either union or friction within our relationships.

Values Drive Your Behaviour, Whether You're Aware of Them or Not

It wasn't until I was thirty-two, and miserable in my job, that I stumbled across a values exercise.

It was an incredibly beautiful day in Toronto, with a crisp blue sky dotted with puffy white clouds. I was walking my dog, Lupa, at Riverdale Park and people were relaxing on the grass all around me, kids were tumbling after each other up and down the hill, and birds were chirping.

I was the vice president of business development for a mid-sized consulting firm that focused on leadership training, coaching, and assessment. I loved my workplace. My colleagues were fantastic, the environment was entrepreneurial and fast-paced (which suited me well), and my boss was great.

But as I looked across the city, a shadow thought about work passed through my mind. My breathing felt tight and a wave of unbelievable sadness passed over me. I felt like I was going to cry.

I walked home and shared my experience with my husband, who works in mental health. "It sounds like you had a panic attack," he said. *Panic attack?!*

For the previous twelve months, I'd been chronically stressed but trying to ignore it. I had started sweating through layers of clothing, including suits. Then I started breaking out in large hive-like welts. I had severe insomnia, and was feeling lost, sad, and overwhelmed.

I couldn't understand why this was happening when the company I was working for was a fantastic fit for me. As head of sales, I felt a great deal of pressure to deliver on our annual budget, but I'd been in leadership roles for several years by that point and had worked in much more challenging situations.

I decided to talk to my boss about what was going on and share that I was struggling. I had no idea what his response would be, but I knew that I needed to shift something. The conversation shifted the course of my career. He listened and empathized and then said, "I've got an idea. Why don't you pilot this new 'career management' coaching program for us? It might help you figure out what's going on and it would help us see if it's a service worth offering our clients."

The premise of the approach—the Q5 Framework, developed by Jay Scherer—was that employees and employers need to find "shared success" in order to maintain engagement and alignment. A key exercise involved doing a deep dive into my personal values: I discovered that one of my driving values was an extremely high need for independence, freedom, and autonomy.

In previous jobs, I had been responsible for everything from sales to marketing to budgeting, and everything in between. In my current role as head of sales, I was responsible for the full P&L of our organization but not all the elements underneath. I had to work closely with the head of consulting (who brought in the talent I had to sell) and the head of marketing (who drove how we marketed our business). Although both were great colleagues, there was friction for me when we didn't align on strategies, which was leading to stress on my end given the self-imposed responsibility I felt towards the overall budget.

I now understood why I was so unhappy. In my existing role, I was never going to get enough autonomy to be satisfied because of the structure.

I was nervous about sharing this insight with my boss. As I considered the framework of the organization, I couldn't see a role that would give me what I now realized I needed. I also knew that unless I shared what I learned; nothing was going to change. Over a couple of conversations, my boss came back to me with a perfect solution. Our open enrollment business had been floundering for a decade. "Why don't you take that on and see if you can turn it around or find a way to sell it?"

Managing the open enrollment business gave me the autonomy I craved and the leadership role that he wanted me to maintain. I loved the challenge of trying to figure out what I could do to turn things around. My panic attacks stopped, my perspiration challenges disappeared, and I was finally sleeping through the night again.

Understanding your values is the crucial first stage in managing your career path.

Your values represent your compass, your internal "true north."

Your core values will drive your behaviour whether you recognize it or not. A value is something that gives us emotional energy and therefore, we tend to do things that move us towards that feeling. Our values develop from the time we are young and, although they may shift over time, there are a few core values that, in my experience, tend to be fairly hardwired.

For me, the need for autonomy was rooted in a childhood where I was the eldest, and the only girl, with three younger brothers. I had my own room, never had to share my toys, and was raised by parents who felt it was important for me to be independent. Throughout my career, I was always pushing for high degrees of autonomy. Ultimately, it's this value that led me out of the corporate world and into entrepreneurship—and it's the same value that makes my mother complain that I don't call her enough!

When our values aren't aligned at work—or in life—we can feel disengaged, unsatisfied, and even stressed out. The good news is that you often don't need to do a major overhaul to fix things. Sometimes all it takes is a few tweaks.

Exercise: Discover Your Values

Grab a journal and be ready to jot down your thinking.

Think of two to three peak life experiences you've had. These are times in your life when you were incredibly happy. What were you doing? What made that moment so great? Who were you with? Write these down with as much detail as possible.

What was it about those moments that made them so joyful? What patterns do you see emerging? Capture them in a few words.

Think of a couple of situations in your life where you or someone you know did something that made you really unhappy or upset. What happened? What was it about the situation that was so upsetting? Now, what patterns do you notice? Do you see any connections between the positive experiences and the times when you were unhappy? Often when we are unhappy, it's because one of our core values is not being met or, as I like to say, "is being stepped on." I once experienced my independence / freedom / autonomy value being "stepped on" when I worked for an organization where the manager was fixated on the employees being at their desks between the required hours of 8:30 and 5:30, regardless of how early you had arrived or how late you stayed the night before. I found the experience suffocating as a senior leader.

Here's a list of values. Note the ones that align to the stories you've just reflected on. Ultimately, you want to shorten your list down to the three to four values that matter to you most. Your non-negotiables.

Values List

Achievement	Health
Activity / Fast Pace	Helping Others
Advancement	Humour
Adventure	Influence
Authenticity	Integrity
Autonomy	Justice
Career Challenge	Leisure
Change and Growth	People Contact
Compensation / Wealth	Personal Development
Competition	Precision Work
Creativity / Innovation	Recognition
Community	Security
Fairness	Stability
Family	Status
Fitness	Teamwork
Flexibility	Variety
Friendship	Work-Life Balance
Fun	Work Under Pressure

Understanding Your Values Will
Help You Make Better Decisions

Over the years, I've interviewed more than a hundred senior leaders on various leadership topics. One of the things I'm always curious about is how they've managed adversity. Whether it was one CEO telling me about how he had to shut down a plant, or another talking about the decision to merge his company with a competitor, or a senior executive talking about a tough decision to lay off staff, when I asked them how they got through these tough situations, I always got the same answer: "I listened to my values."

At the end of the day, especially when you're making tough calls, you will need to be able to look at yourself in the mirror and feel good about the work you've done.

For a lot of mid-career leaders, especially smart, talented ones like you, knowing your values—your non-negotiables—can really help you make smarter career decisions. It becomes much easier to turn down that tempting promotion that doesn't align with how you want to live your life.

Values Can Shift over Time, but Your
Core Values Are Fairly Consistent

People often ask me if values can shift over the years. From my personal experience, and from what I've seen working with clients, my answer is both yes and no.

Life stage and situations can cause some values to become more important. When I was nineteen, my parents moved from Canada back to England where I was born. I was halfway through college, so decided to stay here to complete school. When I was in my early twenties and living alone, my "security" value was very high. I made my education and career choices based on whether those paths would ensure my ability to pay my rent. Once I gained a degree of confidence in my career and earning potential, that value became less of a driver in my career choices. In fact, I've taken several roles at a lower salary because my "change and growth" value was driving my decisions more than any "security" value ever could.

I've never met a senior leader who hasn't identified "health" as a core value, usually because an event has rocked their confidence in this area. Younger leaders don't typically list "health" unless they've had their own wake-up call. When you look at your four core values, chances are you will see threads that tie back to your childhood. In my own observation, our core values don't change that much. You'll know you've really hit a core value if you can say it matters to you in both your professional and personal life. Take some time to do this exercise and revisit it regularly.

Aligning Your Career and Your Values

Once you understand what your core values are, reflect on how well your job is aligned to them.

For Roundtable member Steven, onboarding into a new role was stretching him too thin. Twelve- to sixteen-hour days—plus interruptions by clients all weekend—were wearing him down. Steven's personal values are family, achievement, loyalty, and helpfulness. Although work was benefiting from his loyalty and push to achieve, his family was being severely neglected.

With a visit from his parents on the horizon, and their looming expectations that he would be home immediately after work to spend time with them, the imbalance was becoming too much. Steven was beginning to question whether or not he was cut out for his role.

The process of identifying his values helped him realize he needed to create better boundaries to protect his family value. He ended up negotiating some agreements with his boss around when he would be available to clients and when he would be completely offline.

Setting boundaries helped him reduce the internal pressures he was placing on himself, and allowed his family value to come into better alignment. It wasn't perfect, but he knew that there was a light at the end of the tunnel, and that he would be able to bring even more balance back once his onboarding period was over.

Your values are the foundation from which the rest of your career will grow. Think about them carefully and, when things aren't going well, reflect on how the situation may not be in alignment with your values. Nine times out of ten, if you're unhappy at work, it's usually values related.

📖 Values Session Playbook

Session Length, 70–90 minutes

Timing	Activity
5 minutes	• Leader welcomes group.
10 minutes	• Group provides updates on one success and one learning since the last meeting.
45 to 60 minutes, Values Discussion	• Where are your values currently aligned with the work you're doing? • Where are you feeling a values "rub" or disconnect? • What can you do to create more alignment between your work and your values? • How might you use this exercise with your team?
10 minutes	• Discuss next session pre-work. • Each person shares one key commitment to be completed by next session.
5 minutes	• Wrap Up

☆ CHAPTER 8 HIGHLIGHTS

- Your values are an internal compass that can support your career and life decisions.

- Behaviours tend to be driven by values (whether we're aware of them or not).

- Your work may not support all of your core values fully so seek ways to balance your values outside of your workplace life.

↓ Downloads Available for Chapter 8
- Values exercise
- Stop, start, continue worksheet
- Accountability template
- Session agenda

9

Find Your Zone of Genius

N *FIRST BREAK ALL THE RULES*, co-authors Marcus Buckingham and Curt Coffman note that managers who help people work to their strengths versus forcing them to learn "remedial" activities have higher levels of performance. For example, if you've always been disorganized, chances are all the time management systems and organizational strategies in the world are never going to make you a towering example of organizational excellence. Instead, you'll probably end up being slightly better than average if you really work at it. And who really wants to work at something that drains their energy and only ends up being average?

The strengths-based philosophy asserts that if you focus on your weaknesses (which is what nine out of ten performance reviews do), you will never get "great," instead, you will get "not bad." But if you focus on how to get people to do more work that they're actually great at, performance skyrockets.

Before reading *First Break All the Rules*, I assumed that a strength was something I was really good at. At the time, I was good at several parts of my job, so couldn't figure out why I was miserable.

Here's the secret: a strength is more than just what you're good at, it's something that you love to do. A true strength juices you up and gives you energy.

A common challenge is that most of us have followed a traditional path into the workplace, and we're not rewarded for using our true strengths. In school, we're rewarded for our intellectual ability to meet the marking criteria. Most mainstream schools don't hand out As for an ability to influence others, think on our feet, or build consensus, for example.

It's little wonder that most high school graduates don't know what to major in when going to university, or that many end up dropping out or switching majors. Many people end up compromising and following a path laid out by their parents, teachers, or guidance counsellors. I know I certainly fell into that trap.

In tenth grade, my art teacher said to me "you should go into advertising illustration." That's all I needed to hear. As someone who was on a full-blown mission to move out of the house and get a job, this offered the perfect solution. I liked to draw, so the thought of skipping grade thirteen (the college-prep year in Ontario) and heading straight to college was appealing. It was a bit of a bummer when, by December of my first year, I realized that being an illustrator was definitely *not* my thing. I had the capability but not the passion.

Well-intentioned but misplaced advice and input from others can set us off on paths that aren't the right ones.

In *The Big Leap*, Gay Hendricks refers to that sweet spot between what you love to do and what you're good at as your "zone of genius." I love this expression. Hendricks also asserts that true happiness can be found when we lean into this zone of genius on a regular basis.

There are two ways to establish your zone of genius. The first way is to pinpoint your values because, as we learned in the previous chapter, our values drive our behaviour. In other words, we're more likely to engage in things that we enjoy.

The second way is to start paying attention to the activities you do in your week that give you energy versus the ones that drain your energy. Often, it's not just the activity itself but also the people and environment in which you were doing it.

One of my strengths is public speaking. I particularly love moderating panels and speaking when I can be loose, improvise, and feed off the audience. I get energy from being creative and thinking on my feet. Although I'm good at giving keynote presentations, I don't enjoy them as much. When I need to have a highly scripted approach, I always worry about my tendency to ad lib. If the timeline is tight, I feel too suffocated.

Exercise: Find Your Zone of Genius

As Hendricks says, we all have zones of competence and excellence, but when we work from our zone of genius, magic happens. Figuring out your own zone of genius is a critical part of managing your leadership career successfully.

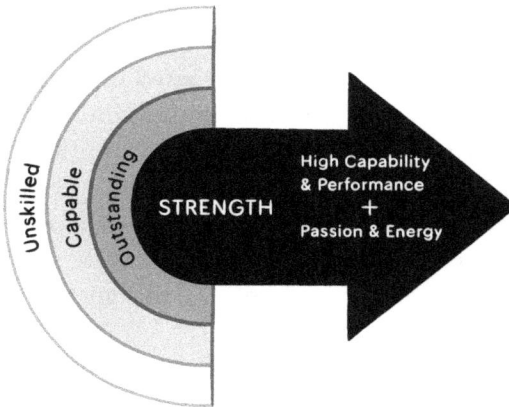

To help you pinpoint your own zone of genius, try monitoring your activities and energy levels for a week:

	Activities that energized me	Activities that drained me
Monday		
Tuesday		
Wednesday		
Thursday		
Friday		
Saturday		
Sunday		

Review your activities. What patterns do you notice? How do these activities connect to your values? What would you like to be doing more of, that you're not currently doing?

Defining Your Zone of Genius Will Help You Manage Your Leadership Career

My very first job was working for the *Ottawa Citizen*, a daily newspaper. I was being completely under-utilized and had an idea for a role I could take on that would juice me up and, I felt, would help the company. I shared my plan to talk to my boss about my idea with a colleague who cautioned me against it, saying, "Who are you to tell Peter that you think you should be doing something else? He's your boss."

Fortunately, I didn't listen to that misplaced advice. I had my conversation and was given the opportunity that I wanted. Why? Because what I was proposing was good for the business and good for me. Win-win.

If you know something is going to play to your strengths *and* it's going to benefit the company, what's the worst that can happen if you approach your boss? They say no? At the very least, you'll leave your boss with a clearer understanding of where you want to contribute more.

When you gain clarity on your strengths, what you want to spend your time doing will become even clearer. You can then look for that opportunity in your next role. Which brings us back to a mantra that bears repeating: You simply cannot rely on your manager to manage your career for you.

Roundtable member Antonella recognized that one of her strengths is strategic thinking. She is incredibly adept at taking highly complex activities, thinking through the long-term implications, and simplifying things into concrete, actionable plans. She loves sorting through opportunities to pinpoint what really matters for the long-term. As an HR business partner (HRBP), she found she had few opportunities to do this kind of work. Instead, she was spending most of her time fire-fighting on a variety of tactical people issues.

One day, she heard the senior VP of HR talking about a new performance management program that needed to be rolled out across the country. There were a number of challenges and complexities to the process and the timeline was tight. Antonella knew it was something she could really sink her teeth into.

She brought the opportunity to her peer group to strategize about how to bring her name forward for consideration. After digging into the issue with her group, Antonella gained the confidence she needed to have a direct conversation with her boss about the opportunity. Within a week she was moved off her HRBP role and into the lead role for the performance management project. Getting clear on your strengths provides you with the confidence to ask for what you want. And, as I always say to my daughter, if you don't ask, you don't get.

📖 Strengths Session Playbook

Session Length, 70–90 minutes

Timing	Activity
5 minutes	• Leader welcomes group.
10 minutes	• Group provides updates on one success and one learning since the last meeting.
40 to 60 minutes, Zone of Genius Discussion	• Each individual to share one strength statement (zone of genius area). • Group provides feedback—what they liked about each statement, plus one thing they could do to strengthen their statement or get clearer. • Review reflection questions.
10 minutes, Reflection	• How could you bring more of your zone of genius to your work? • How will you help others tap into their strengths at work? • What are the potential pitfalls to a strengths-based approach?
5 minutes, Wrap Up	• Discuss next session pre-work (brand). • Each person shares one key commitment to be completed by next session.

☆ CHAPTER 9 HIGHLIGHTS

- Your strength is a combination of what you're good at and what you're passionate about.

- By paying attention to where your energy was high versus where it was low, you can begin to pinpoint your strengths.

- Individuals who work with their strengths can produce more than those who work on their weaknesses.

↓ Downloads Available for Chapter 9
- Strengths worksheet
- Accountability template
- Session agenda

10

Boost Your Brand

YOU ALREADY HAVE a brand at work, whether you manage it consciously or not. Since Tom Peters talked about "A Brand Called You" in 1997 for *Fast Company*, the concept of personal branding has gained credibility as a key element to unlocking opportunities. And, certainly, with the rise and accessibility of social media, we all have multiple opportunities to craft and cultivate our brands beyond the walls of our organizations.

Companies invest millions of dollars to create a strong brand. From there, they work to ensure the experiences that people have with their brand are consistent with what they intend.

When it comes to personal branding and your personal brand experience, a similar investment of energy and effort is required. You are a brand manager!

Explore Your Brand

Think of your brand as the intersection of three elements: passion, performance, and perspective.

In order to cultivate a brand that is authentic (and accurate), it's important to really evaluate how you are operating in the world. This includes understanding what gives you energy, which of your talents drive results, and what those around you have come to count on you for.

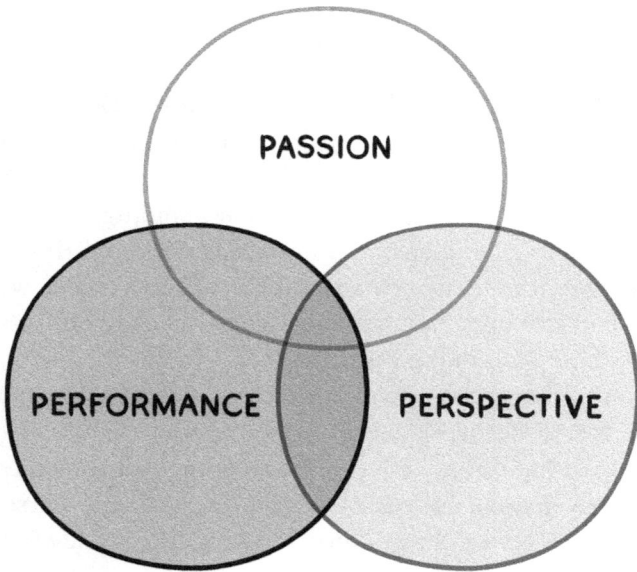

PASSION

PERFORMANCE

PERSPECTIVE

Let's explore what each of these elements means for you. The questions below are designed to spark your thinking and draw out a summary of your key qualities. Grab your journal and work through the questions on the next page.

PASSION

- What "juices" you about your job? What do you enjoy?
- Why is what you do important?
- What are your strengths?
- What are your core values?

PERFORMANCE

- Where can you be counted on for great results?
- What are you known for?
- When faced with an obstacle, what are the "go to" skills you use to overcome it?

PERSPECTIVE

- What is your reputation? How would you describe how people perceive your actions?
- What words best describe you and your leadership style?
- What are the strengths that others consistently acknowledge in you?
- What five words or themes are you seeing come up again and again? List them.

Uncover Your Impact

By exploring your passion, performance, and perspective, you have essentially captured your intentions. Now it's time to see how people around you are experiencing your brand; what is the impact of your brand?

Your brand is a sum of what you are doing (or not doing), saying (or not saying), and how they affect the following:

- What people think when they hear your name.
- What people feel in relation to you.
- What people know about your offering (knowledge, skills, abilities).

The types of experiences you create define your brand in the minds of others, and understanding these experiences will help you find opportunities to build or rebuild your brand.

Remember that those around you ultimately determine your brand by what they see you saying and doing. You can get a sense of what people think about you by reviewing your performance review materials, 360 degree assessment results, or other forms of feedback you may have received over the years. Another great way to get a sense of your brand is to ask those around you for input. Below is an activity that will help you gain some valuable feedback and validate your own perceptions about your reputation.

Brand Survey Instructions:

1. ↓ Download, print, and distribute at least ten copies of the brand survey.

2. Provide to your team, peers, and others who work around you—the more feedback, the better!

3. Ask each person to select and rank the top ten words that describe you. Notice that we've left some blank spaces for you or your colleagues to add words that are also part of your brand.

4. Collect the responses and thank everyone for their input.

Once you've received input from others, identify your key themes. Is there anything you want to change in terms of perceptions of others? What do you want to continue to build into your brand?

Jacqueline's Story

Jacqueline was a senior leader in a large financial institution. She had joined the organization from a much smaller firm two years prior. One of only a handful of women in her division, Jacqueline was interested in seeing how her work colleagues perceived her. In her previous company, she had been known as an approachable, down-to-earth executive, and hoped that she continued to be seen in this light.

After sending out her survey to twenty peers, direct reports, and her boss, some key themes emerged: professional, diplomatic, serious, results-focused, and intelligent. All great words but, for Jacqueline, what was especially insightful were the words that people didn't use to describe her: approachable, friendly, fun, personable.

In her focus to fit into the formality of her new employer and claim her voice in an organization dominated by men, Jacqueline realized that she had lost some of the playfulness and approachability she had always felt was a hallmark of her leadership.

Cultivating Your Brand

For Jacqueline, reestablishing a more informal approach was something that she felt was closer to her authentic leadership self. It's easy to lose track of how we want to show up as leaders given the daily fire-fighting that often occurs in our jobs.

To stay focused, it's helpful to create a brand statement that is simple, memorable, and articulates who you are as a leader.

Consider the following when articulating your brand statement.

Be an Asset, Not a Job Title

- What do you do that brings value?
- What are you most proud of?
- Where do you contribute the most?

Be Authentic so You Can Promote an Honest Brand

- Be honest about your attributes and qualities.
- Focus on who you really are rather than what you think you should be.

Be Distinctive, Stand Apart from the Competition

- What have you done recently to make yourself stand out?
- What would your colleagues or your customers say is your greatest strength?
- What can you say to showcase "you?"
- What would make someone pick you?

As you write your brand statement, remember: you want to stand out from the crowd. Your brand isn't only *what* you do, it's *how* you do it. Many people might be good at "strategic thinking," but what is your "special sauce" that makes the way you think strategically unique?

Here's an example of a brand statement from one of our Roundtable Members:

Cultivator of Relationships. Community Engager and Builder. Professional Elephant Hunter. Renaissance Woman. Shift Disturber.

What does this brand statement tell you about this individual? How would you describe her?

If you said that she's a strong personality, fiercely committed to the people and causes she believes in, and someone who is not afraid to "upset the apple cart," you'd be right.

Notice how her brand statement creates a clear and memorable picture. That's the goal for you too!

Author Seth Godin states: "You have to take control of your brand. Many of us are taught to do our best and then let the world decide how to judge us. I think it's better to do your best and decide how you want to be judged."

When it comes to personal branding, you are in control.

Keep in mind, personal branding is not a one-time event. As our careers and lives evolve, so will our brands. Situations in our organizations shift and change, so we too may need to shift and change our brands to stay relevant.

You will naturally evolve as you expand your knowledge, skills, and experience—both personally and professionally. Growth means change. Your personal brand statement should evolve, too. As you go through significant career and life transitions, it will be important to step back and evaluate how your brand is holding up and what, if anything, you want to do to realign your brand image.

📖 Brand Session Playbook

Session Length, 70–90 minutes

Timing	Activity
5 minutes	• Leader welcomes group.
10 minutes	• Group provides updates on one success and one learning since the last meeting.
40 to 60 minutes, Boost Your Brand Discussion	• Share personal brand statements. • Group provides feedback—what did you like about the individual's statement, plus what is one thing they could do to strengthen their statement?
10 minutes, Reflection	• What can you do to build your brand inside and outside your organization? • How can you maintain consistency in all your actions (and inaction) with your brand? • What networks do you want to expand your brand into? • Where can you inspire, contribute, and share your expertise to build your brand? • How will you revisit and refine your brand as you / your career evolves?
5 minutes, Wrap Up	• Discuss next session pre-work (group decides). • Each person share one key commitment to be completed by next session.

☆ CHAPTER 10 HIGHLIGHTS

- You have a brand whether you recognize it or not.

- Your brand is more than "what" you do; it's "how" you do it.

- Be prepared to adjust and adapt your brand based on the needs of the market.

↓ Downloads Available for Chapter 10
- Brand survey
- Brand statement boosters
- Accountability template
- Session agenda

11

Craft a Kick-Ass Career Vision

ONE OF THE most annoying quotes about careers is "If you do what you love, you'll never work a day in your life." Um, not true! I do what I love and there are many days that feel like a whole lot of work. The difference is that those days are not very frequent and, when they do come up, I'm highly aware of what's bugging me and what I need to do to fix it.

I've noticed that many people stumble into roles and then allow themselves to get swept up into career paths set out for them by their managers, parents, or peers. I've coached many people who find themselves in big, sexy, well-paid roles but feel completely empty on the inside.

As leaders, we have an absolute responsibility to find a career that makes us feel fulfilled. After all, if we're not happy, how are we going to help others on our teams find their career joy?

But here's the thing: your dream career simply isn't going to land in your lap. Instead, you need to get intentional about creating the career you want. I've always pictured my career happiness like one of those old radios where you have to twist the dial to find a station with good reception. When we're miserable in our career, everything can sound like static. Then, as we start to tune in to the activities and areas that give us joy, we find ourselves moving towards jobs that make us sing versus those that make us crazy.

As leaders, we have the opportunity to impact the lives of those around us daily, and having a well-articulated career plan will help us ground ourselves in our purpose, or "why," around leadership.

In this chapter, we'll look at how to create an inspiring career vision for ourselves. Then, in chapter 12, we'll look at the two key kinds of goals we'll need to set to achieve that vision: knowledge / skill goals and behaviour goals.

There are three exercises as part of your pre-work for this session. Your group should complete them in advance so that you can use your time together to really dive into what you've created in order to support and hold each other accountable. This chapter outlines an overview of each of the exercises and what you can expect from each one so that you can guide the discussion.

Where Are You Now?

Creating a career vision can feel really overwhelming. This was true for Julie. As head of marketing for a global multinational company, Julie spent most of her twenties and early thirties with her head down and her vision firmly focused on the next rung of the career ladder.

When the topic of writing a career vision came up, she felt completely stuck and could only focus on the next role that she could see ahead of her, the next rung on the ladder. The problem was, she wasn't really sure it was the role she wanted. She felt lost.

One of the best ways to get "unstuck" is to start by inventorying the skills and abilities you have, and which of those things you enjoy and would like to do more of, and which you'd rather do less of (even though you may be good at them). You can reference the exercises you did to determine your zone of genius in chapter 8 to help you here. These are some of the things Julie came up with.

Julie's Inventory

Skills and Abilities	Do I want to do more of this type of work / activity?	Would I rather do less of this type of work / activity?
Strong experience in traditional consumer marketing.		Yes—want to focus on digital marketing more than traditional approaches.
Solid presentation skills.	Yes—with more senior people.	
Good at building teams and coaching team members.	Yes—enjoy developing others.	
Creative thinker and able to conceptualize solutions quickly.	Yes—like new ideas and would enjoy opportunities to do this beyond the marketing function.	
Strong at data analysis.		Yes—would prefer to operate at a higher level.

By inventorying your current role, you will start to isolate the activities that you want to build into your career vision.

It's Your Future, So Dream Big

Reflecting on our careers allows us to be better prepared for creating our longer-term vision. Perhaps members of your group feel like they're not "planners" and that they're "not good at setting goals." Or maybe the problem is that they're not good at sticking to goals, once defined.

There are two exercises to help you build a longer-term career vision. The first activity is a "Retirement Party" vision. You could also write your obituary (as in chapter 6), but this approach is a little less morbid. The retirement exercise allows you and your group to move away from the reality of the day-to-day, and instead consider how you want to be thought of as your career wraps up. Julie's is below.

Julie's Retirement Party Vision

What types of activities have you been doing during your final year before retirement? (Don't think about your title or where you're working, think about how you would be spending your days.)

I love mentoring others and I see myself teaching, and possibly doing more writing. I've always had a goal to write a book based on my experience in marketing. I'd love to still be working with a team of people, but I think I'd like to be closer to the action. Perhaps part of a smaller company where I could really be making an impact by being on the executive team.

What Are People Saying about Your Contributions at Work?

People talk about how I made a difference by taking risks. I was always up for doing something out of the box and on the cutting edge. I encouraged my team to try and fail. I was able to really make an impact in my organization.

What Are People Saying about Your Leadership Style and Impact?

People say I'm a kind leader and excellent coach. I put my team first and am remembered as someone who supported my people every step of the way.

How Will You Spend Your Days as a Retired Professional?

I see myself travelling more and volunteering for causes I believe in, like animal welfare. I will continue to be physically active and would like to be able to "give back" to the marketing community through writing and mentoring other young professionals.

AS YOU CAN see from Julie's answers, there are some key themes that she can focus on as she creates her career vision. As you write your own responses, go back and look for your key themes.

Your Three-Year Career Vision

The second exercise to help you build out your vision is to bring things a little closer to home. Keeping your retirement picture in mind, think about what your career and life will look like in three years.

Three years is far enough away that you have time to build towards it, but not so far away that it feels out of reach. In Jim Collins's masterful book *Good to Great*, he notes that winning companies create a Big Hairy Audacious Goal (BHAG). This goal often seemed outrageous and impossible, yet winning companies have used them as inspiration, and as a compass to create momentum and ultimately success.

I want you to create your own Big Hairy Audacious Career Vision—a BHAC Vision! As you write it, don't think about "how" you'll get to where you want to go, instead focus on the vision itself. When we think about "how" we'll do things, we end up editing ourselves. We start to get stuck in what feels realistic and what doesn't. This is a time to let yourself dream.

It is important to think holistically. Consider the experiences you want to have, the work you want to do, and the people you want to interact with. Consider how you'll be spending your free time, what you'll be doing outside of work. Remember, work and life are interconnected. It may be helpful to think about your career vision in specific areas: type of work, financial reward, status, family, friends, health. The key is not to limit yourself. Be bold! Have fun! I highly recommend finding a quiet spot with your favourite beverage to complete this exercise.

Pro tip: As you write your BHAC Vision, articulate it as if it's already happened.

Excerpt from Julie's Three-Year Big Hairy Audacious Career Vision

Three years from now, I still work in marketing and have dug even deeper into digital marketing and data analytics. I have completed my MBA and have taken on a bigger team that is giving me even more experience with managing across divisions.

I volunteer for one high-profile committee within the organization that gives me increased exposure to senior level leaders. I completed an advanced coaching and leadership skills workshop and have built a reputation as a leader that people want to work with. There is always an abundance of people applying to open roles on my team.

I bought a condo downtown, which I love, and am able to travel extensively. I use up my vacation time every year, I never take my laptop or phone with me, and have travelled to Hawaii, Australia, and India.

My personal life is flourishing. I make regular visits back home to see my parents, and spend lots of time with family and friends. I have met my life partner and am planning my wedding.

I have maintained my fitness goals and have completed my first marathon.

Once you have your career vision in place, your next step will be to nail down some specific goals to get you there. Be ready to share your vision with your group.

📖 Career Vision Session Playbook

Session Length, 75–95 minutes

Timing	Activity
5 minutes	• Leader welcomes group.
10 minutes	• Group provides updates on one success and one learning since the last meeting.
40 to 60 minutes, Individual Goal Share– 15 minutes per person	• 5 minutes: read retirement vision to group. • 5 minutes: share BHAC Vision. • 5 minutes: group Q&A to help each group member dig deeper and get really specific about their vision.
10 minutes, Reflection	• How easy / hard was it to create your career vision? • What was it like to share this vision out loud with the rest of the group? • What changes / adjustments (if any) do you want to make to your career vision?
10 minutes, Wrap Up	• Discuss next session pre-work (group setting). • Each person shares one commitment to be completed by the next session.

☆ CHAPTER 11 HIGHLIGHTS

- A well-articulated leadership vision allows us to make short-term career decisions clearly and easily.

- Breaking down your vision into a three-year horizon is far enough out that it's a stretch, but not so far out that it feels unreachable.

- If we don't know where we're going, we may end up in a place we don't want to be.

↓ Downloads Available for Chapter 11
- Visioning exercise
- Accountability template
- Session agenda

Set Goals
that Matter

N OW THAT YOU and your group members have created some kick-ass career visions, it's time to nail down some shorter-term goals to get you there.

Before we set our goals, here's a fun fact on why crafting a vision is useful: when you attach your goals to a clear vision, you're actually moving your thinking up into the motivation centres, or the executive function, of the brain. You get a lot more excited when you're clear on your "why."

Goals tend to break down into two main categories:

1. Knowledge and skills you need to acquire.

2. Behaviours you need to build.

Most performance development plans I've reviewed tend to focus on outcomes that people need to achieve (e.g., sales results, project deadlines, cost savings) or knowledge or skills they need to acquire (e.g., improve presentation skills, get an industry certification, learn about a new part of the business).

It's no wonder most of us find ourselves feeling a bit scattered when it comes to our career paths. We're fully focusing on the short-term goals that matter primarily to the organization we work for, not for ourselves personally.

Your group members should complete the activities outlined here in advance of your session.

How to Set Goals

Strong goals should be specific, important, and measurable (SIM) steps to get started. Here are some examples of SIM goals:

Not SIM	SIM Goal
Increase my influence skills	Get two of my ideas to increase department efficiency approved by senior management before year-end.
Increase my visibility	Join a not-for-profit board by [insert date] and volunteer to chair the [insert name], annual sales committee conference in [insert date].
Manage my temper	Have no incidences where I have to apologize for losing my temper between now and the end of the year.

Knowledge and Skill Goals: What Do You Need to Learn?

Knowledge goals and skill goals tend to be easy for most people to articulate and achieve. They usually fall into the categories of things you need to learn or experiences you need to have. Based on Julie's three-year BHAC Vision, she came up with these top three SIM goals:

- Enroll in my MBA in June of this year. (Knowledge)
- Increase coaching skills by participating in the internal mentoring program as a mentor starting in September. (Skill)
- Engage with a real-estate agent to begin looking for a condo to purchase by the end of this month. (Knowledge)

With knowledge and skill goals in place, it's time to tackle the goal that is usually the one that makes and breaks most leaders' careers: the behaviour goal.

Behaviour Goals: How Are You Showing Up?

Early in my career, I took a management 101 program and had the good fortune to learn from a professor called Monte Christie (not even joking). He made the analogy that, as leaders, when we join an organization we begin to grow a tail. The tail grows with each decision we make and each behaviour we demonstrate. He said that when you look around an organization, you will see people with strong, firm tails and others with scraggly, ragged tails. Everyone can see your tail. These tails become labels.

"When you know better, you do better."

MAYA ANGELOU
American poet

We label people in order to know what to expect from them, and how to deal with them. "John's always late." "Phil is often short-tempered." "Shameen is ambitious."

If you want someone to see you differently—or change their view of your "tail"—you need to start shifting their perception by changing your behaviours and making sure they see those changes. In the previous chapter you thought about how you want to be remembered at your retirement party. Chances are your description is chock full of behaviours that you demonstrated.

Let's take a look again at Julie's retirement goal for what she wanted people to say about her, with attention to the behaviours she wants to be remembered for demonstrating.

People say I'm a kind leader and excellent coach. I put my team first and am remembered as someone who supported my people every step of the way.

How would you define "kindness?" What are the behaviours that make up being an "excellent coach?" How would we evaluate Julie as a leader who "put her team first" and "supported" her people?

Behaviour, in a nutshell, can be broken down into the things we *say* and the things we *do*.

As you consider your own vision statement, which behaviours stand out for you? Are there some that are natural for you to demonstrate consistently? Are some aspirational? Do you demonstrate these behaviours consistently—even when you're under stress? What do you *say* and *do* on a regular basis that demonstrates these behaviours?

Most of us are clear on the aspects of our leadership approach that we do well, and the aspects that we need to work on. Our performance reviews are usually filled with "opportunity areas," many of which you may see repeated year after year. Here's a list of typical goals I see during our Roundtable programs that come from these performance reviews or manager feedback.

- Get better at listening.
- Learn to let go of control.
- Delegate more.
- Manage my emotions when under pressure.
- Increase my influence with _____.
- Be more strategic.
- Get better at dealing with ambiguity.

Ironically, for seasoned, successful leaders, the behaviour that we usually need to work on is often the dark side of one of our greatest strengths.

Here's an example: Gerald was the finance director in his multinational organization. One of his towering strengths was his ability to gain input from others. In his performance review feedback, he was commended for this ability to manage competing agendas and solicit everyone's feedback to make better decisions. In the same performance review, Gerald's opportunity area was to be more "decisive" and take a more independent stand. His use of consensual and collaborative behaviour was a liability in situations that required him to think and act quickly. Indecisiveness was the downside to his upside.

The challenge for Gerald—and for all of us—is to figure out when our strengths become liabilities and then use different behaviours in those situations.

Let's go back to Julie. Her goal to be a kind leader who supports her people is admirable. But as she reviewed her performance feedback, she recognized a pattern: her boss continually called out her need to be more direct in giving feedback. She was perceived as being soft and not firm enough with underperformers. Her kindness and empathy were actually becoming her biggest leadership liabilities, and putting her next promotion in question.

Leaders have to be courageous and initiate tough conversations. Julie found it difficult to strike a balance between pushing her team for results, and caring for their feelings. She often found herself taking on extra work herself instead of "burdening" her colleagues with that work.

Here are some other examples of when strengths can become weaknesses. See if any feel familiar to you.

Strength	When overused
Comfortable with change	Creates chaos due to lack of focus
Strategic thinker	Slow to seize opportunities
Passionate	Intense
Decisive	Doesn't always listen well
Collaborative	Slow to make decisions
Results-oriented	Creates too much pressure
Kind and empathetic	Avoids conflict
Delegates	Too hands off
Good with process	Inflexible
Follows up on plans	Micromanages

It's easier to "start" a new behaviour than "stop" an old behaviour.

Get Intentional: It's All about Micro-Behaviours

The best way to build a new behaviour is to start small and *do one thing consistently*. Over time, that *one thing* will become a habit, and these small, simple actions—or micro-behaviours—will create a new "go-to behaviour" in your toolkit.

As you think about your own plan, don't think big—think small! I find when we start talking about behaviours, people often feel like they need to make some major shift. This isn't the case: it's often very simple things that result in a big bang for your buck. In fact, at The Roundtable, we encourage clients to choose one "big bang for your buck" behaviour™ to work on.

Here's an example: one of my clients, we'll call her Manon, was a type-A, results-oriented driver. Her 360 feedback revealed that people found her intimidating. She wanted to change that perception.

The first place to start when it comes to shifting other people's perception of you is to leverage an approach popularized by Marshall Goldsmith called FeedForward. (You will find a full description of how to do FeedForward on page 142 in chapter 14.)

With FeedForward, you ask your key stakeholders what you can do to start demonstrating a new behaviour. In Manon's case, she spoke to her boss, peers, and direct reports and got each of their "one best suggestion" on what she could start doing in order to appear more approachable. By getting input from these stakeholders, Manon wasn't simply "guessing" at what they needed to see. She was, instead, getting the straight goods. One of the pieces of feedback that she received from her direct reports and boss was that she would go directly to her office in the mornings and shut the door. This led people around her to conclude that she was in a bad mood, and they were often afraid to interrupt her. She was also told that she didn't smile very much.

Now, these things might seem ridiculously minor, but this is my point. Most changes you will need to make are not that big. For Manon, who tended to be very business focused, slowing down and smiling and chatting with people on her way to her desk was something that had never occurred to her as being important. Once she became aware of people's expectations, she was able to get intentional about slowing down and smiling on her way to her desk each morning.

And this is really the key. To make a new behaviour stick, you must be consistent and apply it with intention. This often feels like we're not being "authentic." That's normal. Practicing a new behaviour is going to feel strange. We feel like we are "faking it until we make it" because we have to think about our approach and how we plan to use the new behaviours. Stick with it! Over time that new behaviour will become easier and more effortless.

One of the best ways to turn your micro-behaviours into habits is to create a set of five daily questions that you ask yourself at the start and end of each day.

Come up with five prompts or intentions for the day. Think of it as an affirmation. Let's go back and take a look at the Daily Top Five Julie created to become more direct and results-driven with her direct reports.

Today, I am going to do my best to:

1. Provide one piece of positive feedback to my direct reports.

2. Provide constructive feedback in the moment.

3. Be direct in expressing my expectations to others at my initial meeting on a new project.

4. Follow up immediately to make sure my expectations were clear.

5. Provide specific details on what worked and what didn't at the end of meetings.

Practicing a new behaviour can feel awkward and uncomfortable, but remember: no growth ever happens in our comfort zones. With focus, consistent practice, and continued feedback, anyone with the will to change can add new behaviours to their toolkits.

Here's the Bad News

While it's true that small, incremental changes applied consistently can have a massive impact, your chances of making behavioural change overnight are not high.

Have you ever decided to get fit? Lose weight? Launch a side hustle? Only to stay out of shape, gain weight, and never get to the hustle? It's easy to set goals, hard to follow through on them. We get distracted. Other "priorities" creep in. And when it comes to creating a new behaviour and keeping our leadership plans on track, it is *really* easy to get sucked into the daily minutiae and complexity of leading in today's volatile, uncertain, complex, and ambiguous (VUCA) world.

So, what can you do to bulletproof your plans? You leverage your peer group to help you stay accountable. Each time your group gets together from this point onwards, use the opportunity to provide an update on how you're doing against your goals. If you and your group members work together in the same organization, ask them to watch for your new behaviours in action. This accountability and encouragement will be key to helping you stay on track. And remember, according to research done by Marshall Goldsmith, individuals who do consistent follow-up around their actions with their stakeholders are perceived to have made more progress, so be sure to circle back to your stakeholders a few months into your new approach to make sure they can see your "new tail."

📖 Goal Setting Session Playbook

Session Length, 75–90 minutes

Timing	Activity
5 minutes	• Leader welcomes group.
10 minutes	• Group provides updates on one success and one learning since the last meeting.
45 to 60 minutes, Individual goal share– 15 minutes per person	• 5 minutes: recap BHAC Vision. • 5 minutes: share top 3 goals. • 5 minutes: group members provide "feedforward" suggestions to build out action plans.
10 minutes, Reflection	• What did you notice about the goals that the group shared? Were there commonalities or differences? • How would you like the group to support you in your goals? • What is one thing you would like to accomplish around your goals between now and your next group session?
10 minutes, Wrap Up	• Discuss next session pre-work. • Each person shares one key commitment to be completed by next session.

☆ CHAPTER 12 HIGHLIGHTS

- Behaviour is often the barrier to future career possibilities.

- For successful people, overusing strengths creates liabilities.

- To change behaviour, small intentional changes are required—keep it simple and go for the "big bang for the buck."

↓ Downloads Available for Chapter 12
- Macro goals template
- Feedforward primer
- Micro-behaviour worksheet
- Accountability template
- Session agenda

FOUR

Perform

13

Decision Point
Moving Forward

T SOME POINT, your group may be ready to wrap things up. Some members may want to transition to other development experiences, or they have simply gained what they needed from the group experience. Many groups can find themselves simply fading away. I think this is a missed opportunity for learning and connection. If you're ready to wrap up, page 135 of this chapter will give you some ideas on how to close off your group experience with intention.

If you're not sure where group members stand in terms of continuing or wrapping up, below are some thoughts on how to discuss your options, as well as some ways you can revamp the group if you want to change things up a bit.

1. Who is interested in continuing on with the group?

- Do we want to continue with the format as-is?

2. If we want to change things up:

- What do we want to keep?

- What changes do we want to make?
- What is the right schedule for the group?

3. If some members are departing:

- Do we want to add group members?
- What will be our process for onboarding?
- What term do we want to keep meeting for (six months / one year / other)?

With this input, you will be able to come up with a new plan for your group going forward. Here are some of the changes that have worked within The Roundtable community for groups that opt to continue on:

1. **Less frequent meetings:** Many groups that try and stick to a four- to six-week schedule following the formal program find it challenging. Instead, groups who meet quarterly, or even twice per year, sometimes get improved turnout and better results.

2. **Nominate new members:** To ensure a good fit, most groups opt to have new members join by being nominated by existing members. New potential members meet with other group members for coffee and, if there is consensus, will be invited into the group. If you are onboarding a new group member, don't forget to incorporate one of the "getting to know you" activities outlined on page 47 and redo your confidentiality agreements to accelerate the trust within the newly established group.

3. **Rotating leaders:** To ensure that group leadership is shared, successful groups divide meeting tasks between group members to ensure the job of coordinating communications and agendas doesn't fall to one person. This increases the likelihood of ongoing success.

That's All Folks! Wrapping Up

All good things must come to an end. Your final session provides your group with an opportunity to step back and reflect on the journey you've made, the experiences you've had, and the goals you've achieved.

It's important to put a final "bow" on your experience. Any good leadership coaching journey incorporates the measurement of progress on goals, and the opportunity to consolidate learning.

If your group decides that it's time to call things a wrap, here are a couple of exercises to consider that will allow your group to end intentionally.

Pro tip: Both exercises are best completed in advance of your session, so be sure to provide your group members with the questions and instructions ahead of time.

Group Reflection

A key part of wrapping up your peer coaching experience is providing group members with the space to share their reflections and learnings. Some questions to use as prompts with your group include:

- What have you learned most during your experience in the peer group?

- What contribution did you make to the group that you are most proud of?

- What do you wish you had done differently?

- How did you find the conversations we explored changed your approach to leadership, or changed your approach outside of work?

- What has been your biggest "aha" moment over the course of this experience?

Provide everyone with five minutes to share their thoughts. You can do this "popcorn style" by simply having people speak freely when they're ready, or you can ask someone to volunteer to start and then select the next person who'll speak. Popcorn style often works well with this activity because it allows people to build on each other's thinking.

Group Appreciation

The opportunity to give positive feedback and appreciation is often neglected in organizations. In my observations of fellow leaders, I've noticed that we agonize for hours when we have to give constructive feedback, but will toss off "good job!" to people with abandon. There is a great opportunity with a peer group to not only give our colleagues meaningful feedback, but also practice the lost art of praise.

When it comes to giving meaningful feedback, it's important that we get really specific so that the individual knows exactly why they are appreciated.

Here are two examples of appreciation feedback. Which one do you think has the greater impact on the recipient?

Appreciation message 1: *Andrew, you have a great sense of humour.*

Appreciation message 2: *Andrew, you brought a great sense of humour to our group. I really appreciated how you were able to lighten the mood and made us remember that, although our work is important, it's not always as life and death as we make it out to be. As someone who tends to place a lot of pressure on myself, I have learned a lot from you about the importance of not sweating the small stuff, and find myself laughing about things a lot more than I used to. Thank you.*

Ask for a volunteer to begin the appreciation exercise. You may want to designate a specific "appreciation chair" for the individual to sit in as they receive their feedback.

One by one, group members will read their appreciation message aloud to the person sitting in the appreciation chair. You may want to record the messages on your phone and send the audio file to the group member following the session. Or have people write their response onto slips of paper that can be placed in an envelope for the recipient.

Once the last person has read their message, the individual who has been showered with kind words has an opportunity to say thank you (or anything else they would like). It's important that they not interrupt the speakers while they are receiving the praise, which can be hard for some listeners! It's quite common for members of the group to feel uncomfortable about having to sit quietly and bask in the kind words being sent their way—this exercise often brings some laughter and tears. The recipient will then pick the next person from the group to take their place in the appreciation chair. Continue with this process until everyone has received their appreciation.

Accepting feedback is something that many successful people struggle with, and yet is an important skill to be able to handle with grace. I've seen many successful leaders—including yours truly—who quickly reject and dismiss positive feedback by discounting it or minimizing their accomplishments.

This self-deprecating behaviour becomes less and less endearing the more successful you become. Learning to accept positive accolades, and own your strength and positive impact, is an important part of leadership. After all, if you can't accept a compliment, how can you expect your team to accept yours when you give it to them?

📖 Wrap Up Session Playbook

Session Length, 80 minutes

Timing	Activity
5 minutes	• Leader welcomes group.
10 minutes	• Group provides updates on one success and one learning since the last meeting.
30 minutes, Group Appreciation— 5 minutes per person	• Individual appreciation feedback.
30 minutes, Group Reflection— 5 minutes per person	• What did you gain from this experience personally? • What did you gain from this experience professionally?
5 minutes	• Wrap Up

☆ CHAPTER 13 HIGHLIGHTS

- Reflection is an important component for consolidating a learning experience, so don't skip it.

- Providing concrete and specific appreciation feedback for your fellow group members will deepen their self-insight—and make them feel good!

- Receiving appreciation from group members provides each group member with an opportunity to practice accepting kind words gracefully. (It's amazing how hard this is for many of us to do.)

↓ Downloads Available for Chapter 13
- Reflection and appreciation worksheets
- Session agenda

14

Building Community in the Workplace

ODAY'S LEADERS NEED their own peer groups to help navigate the complexity of leadership, and also to benefit from knowing how to cultivate and grow community within organizations. In peer groups, we have an opportunity to role-model vulnerability, transparency, and connection to our colleagues.

And here's the good news: all the exercises that you've experienced with your peer group are exercises you can use as a leader to build a stronger sense of community within your team. Here are few ways you can get started.

Build Behaviours Together

Create a list of key behaviours that are expected within your team. Your corporate values—if you have them—can be a great place to start. As a team, discuss:

- What's one behaviour we do really well?

- What's one behaviour that collectively we could do better?

- What specific micro-behaviours can we practice getting better at?

- How will we measure success?

Feedforward

Take behaviour change one step further and build a culture of performance by bringing the Feedforward technique into your teams. (For more on the Feedforward technique, read *What Got You Here Won't Get You There* by Marshall Goldsmith.) With your team behaviours in place, ask each team member to choose *one* behaviour that they would like to improve. Then pair up and provide each other with one best suggestion using the Feedforward technique:

1. Share your behaviour.

2. Ask for one best suggestion.

3. Listen.

4. Thank.

5. Follow up to see how others are noticing your behaviour change in action.

Consider making this Feedforward activity something that you do at your team meetings on a quarterly basis to keep the group focused on the behaviours and moving in the right direction.

Explore Values

Probably the most popular activity that participants in our Roundtable for Leaders program take to their teams is the values exercise. If you haven't already tried it with your team, it's a great place to start. Have members complete the values worksheet. In an upcoming one-on-one meeting, explore their values and how they align with the work they're doing.

You can also take it a step further and have a group discussion about values, using the following questions as prompts:

1. Which of your individual values align really well with this team and our broader organization?

2. Is there anywhere you're struggling with a value disconnect?

3. How can we support each other?

Values drive individual behaviour, but they also drive team behaviour. I once worked with an executive team that had a very serious mandate to be innovative and to drive change. When we looked at the collective values of the group, everyone—with the exception of the team leader—had very little energy for change; instead, they valued process and procedure. The group had lots of big ideas, but nothing was getting accomplished because the individuals within the team prioritized their operational roles before the implementation of new ideas. The team's awareness of the gap helped them understand why they were struggling and allowed them to create a plan to move forward.

As leaders, our personal values and the energy they create will definitely shape the teams we lead, so be aware of how you may be unintentionally creating challenges for your people. How do your own values affect your team? Are there aspects of your personal values and motivators that are steering your team in the wrong direction?

Leverage Strengths

The "zone of genius" strength-finder exercise is an excellent activity to do with your team members on a regular basis. With change happening so rapidly, it's incredibly helpful to have a pulse on what your team members' interests are. The foundation of a great career conversation is understanding an individual's strengths and ambitions.

Here are some ways to talk about strengths to you team members:

1. What results or outcomes are you most proud of in your current role? (This question gives insight into what they place value on.)

2. What do you currently enjoy the most about your role?

3. If I could give you more of something, what would that be?

4. If I could give you less of something, what would that be?

These four questions will give you a solid view into your colleague's activities and interests. This type of discussion opens up a much wider set of options—for them and for you—than a very narrow focus on a particular job position or possible promotion.

Build Your Team Brand

Something that team leaders often overlook is the opportunity to galvanize your group under a shared purpose. Members of your team can complete the personal brand-building activities, but you can also apply the same concept to your team as a whole. What will your team be known for? What will be your team's legacy?

Creating a shared vision and purpose for your team gives them energy and moves them beyond the day-to-day activities of your deliverables.

For example, a manufacturing team that we worked with through The Roundtable was struggling in a shared leadership model; it was creating divisiveness between functional leaders, and spawning siloes that were eroding trust and constructive conflict. They were cultivating a brand of a disparate group of competing leaders; they recognized the need to increase collaboration and find ways to work together more effectively. In the time-pressured environment of 24 / 7 operations, they needed a shared purpose to pull competing priorities under one overarching vision. As a leadership group they developed the simple statement as their guiding slogan—Achieve, Collaborate, Today (ACT)—and developed a set of team behaviours that included acting with "all in" as a principle, speaking with one voice, and being bold in their decisions.

The group's goal was to be seen as a cohesive leadership unit, and to change the perceptions that other parts of the organization had about their team brand.

A powerful way to extract yourselves from the day-to-day, and to gain some perspective, is to focus your team on a "North Star," and think "what will people say about us when they look back on our time together?"

Leverage Peer Coaching to Solve Group Issues

Roundtable graduate Tamara was observing lots of friction between three of the teams in her division. She decided to pull the groups together and use The Roundtable Peer Coaching Method to help them work through their challenges. She simplified the framework to focus on more of a problem-solving structure by taking the emphasis off any individual issue, and instead focusing the group on a shared issue.

Tamara tabled the topic, and group members were able to ask her questions to make sure everyone clearly understood the issue. From there, Tamara had group members share their ideas on what they thought would help solve the problem. Once all the ideas were tabled, the group voted on which ideas were the most feasible to act on.

This modified peer coaching / problem-solving structure is now something this group does on a regular basis as a way to deal with sticky issues across teams.

You can also use The Roundtable Peer Coaching Method with your team members for topics that might be more "coachable" than problem-solving. Here are some examples:

- Coaching a team member who has to have a difficult conversation with a customer.

- Coaching a team member who's taking on too much work.

- Coaching a team member who may be feeling tired or burned out.

- Coaching a team member who's struggling with a family issue.

When you group coach with your teams, you allow them to build their coaching skills together while simultaneously learning from each other. You also create a space for vulnerability that increases feelings of connection and community.

As team leader, you're also building your own coaching ability and creating more capacity within your team members to elevate their own skills. Peer coaching is a powerful approach for developing leadership, it will ensure your team members are less isolated and overwhelmed, and more agile and connected.

Conclusion
Leadership and Community

I N 2017, MY daughter and I attended WE Family, an event organized by the charity Me to We to encourage young people to support community initiatives. At the event, Me to We co-founder Marc Kielburger shared a story of building a school in a small mountain community in South America.

The team was struggling to complete the building. Marc was worried that it wouldn't be ready for the opening that was two days away. He shared his fears with one of the village elders. The woman smiled and told him not to worry. They would have a mingar, she said. She then walked over to the edge of the ridge that overlooked the valley. Placing her hands of either sides of her mouth, she called out in a loud, clear voice, "Mingar." It echoed over the valleys, "Mingar, mingar, mingar..."

Marc, confused, returned back to his work with the team. They worked through the night trying to make headway on the project, but by morning they still weren't close to being ready for opening. It wasn't looking good.

And then something happened. People started arriving. Villagers from within the valleys and beyond left their planting, left their chores, left their farming behind. They started to assemble around the school, ready to work.

The elder smiled at Marc. "Mingar," she said.

"Mingar" is a Spanish word that means: "Coming together to support a communal task. The act of working together communally."

In this volatile, uncertain, complex, and ambiguous world, we need community more than ever before.

Technology drives innovation, but it also increases isolation. Human beings are built for connection, and yet "social" media continues to be a factor in the loneliness epidemic. Workplace mental health issues are increasing, and employee engagement continues to plummet. For many of us, our lives revolve around work and the relationships we build there, and yet the pace and pressure of business is causing us to become increasingly transactional.

Researcher and psychologist Naomi Eisenberger, along with other neuroscientists, theorize that a lack of feeling a connection with others creates pain; not only the emotional discomfort of loneliness, but also symptoms analogous to physical pain. In fact, some of the same brain regions that respond to physical pain also respond to "social pain"—the painful feelings associated with social rejection or loss.

For thousands of years, we have formed communities and belonged to groups. Building your own peer group allows you to create a network of support that will be crucial, not just now, but for the rest of your career. Leveraging these skills to build community within your team increases engagement and, in turn, productivity.

In this Age of Collaboration, our leadership impact will be measured to a very large degree on our ability to build and maintain relationships with others. The pace of disruption demands that we understand how to create our own leadership support system, rather than rely on our managers to nurture and take accountability for our career paths.

I hope this book has inspired you to create your own powerful leadership community to support you as you navigate through your career and life stages. The exercises I've outlined can be revisited regularly, with the conversations getting richer each time your group explores them.

Leadership is an ongoing journey of personal discovery, and one that doesn't have to feel lonely or isolating when you have the right people in your corner.

Start your own Grassroots Leadership Revolution today.

The world needs great leaders. The world needs *you*.

References and Resources

Managing the Tricky Bits

Anytime you bring groups of people together, you will encounter some bumps. Though I've only ever had one situation when a leader was "voted off the island" by their group, it can happen.

Mostly, I've noticed that group energy wanes as people's interests and needs shift. Here's my list of some of the key challenges that you may encounter, and how to prevent or problem-solve each one:

Challenges	What you can do . . .
Lack of fit	Lack of chemistry can often come down to one or two people who don't "fit" the rest of the group. Doing more "getting to know you" trust-building exercises can really open a dialogue, but sometimes a person simply does not fit and it's better for them to decide to opt out. As tribe leader, be prepared to have those straight-up conversations. If a bad fit is left unaddressed, it will bring down your entire efforts. Don't ignore the problem, and don't ignore the person in the hope they'll "get the message."

Challenges	What you can do...
Loss of mojo	Group seems to lose energy. This can happen when a group's been together for a while. This might be an opportunity to change up the cadence of group meetings and / or mix up activities. Some of The Roundtable's preferred methods include bringing in a guest speaker, going on field trips to other organizations, and making sure to keep the sessions varied with one-on-one as well as full group discussions.
Discomfort with peer coaching	Sometimes people may not be comfortable being vulnerable with their peers immediately. Others may want to jump right in. It's important to respect each person's level of comfort and provide people with the time / space to reveal what they're comfortable with; however, if someone is unwilling to fully participate and share their own "good, bad, and ugly" with their peers (when their peers are being candid), then it's worth having a one-to-one conversation to see if there's a bigger issue at play.
Lack of commitment	Two of the biggest ways that lack of commitment can sabotage your group coaching program are: • Group members not committing to times or preparing for sessions. • Group members showing up late. In my experience, communicating expectations to all involved at the start is critical, and outlining / enacting consequences is a must. Go back to your ground rules regularly and engage the group in solving any issues that might be emerging.
Confidentiality breach	Most of the time when confidentiality is breached within a group, it's accidental. A group member may make what they think is an innocuous comment, which then snowballs into a confidentiality breach. When this happens, it's easy for the group to lose trust and for group members to start to shut down. Reviewing the confidentiality agreements at the start and end of each session is one way to eliminate this issue before it happens, but if there is a confidentiality breach, it's important to address it immediately and work with the group to find a solution. For most groups, this usually means working through the issue and revisiting their group confidentiality ground rules; for some groups, it may mean asking the person involved to leave.

The Roundtable Peer Coaching Method

STEP 1: HEADLINE

Members share a specific challenge / opportunity that they would like to bring up to the group in one or two sentences (no details).

STEP 2: SELECT

Members prioritize the challenges / opportunity and select one to begin with.

STEP 3: SHARE

One by one, members share their challenge or opportunity in more detail.

STEP 4: COACH

Group members then ask coaching questions (no advice or suggestions) to uncover root issues. See chapter 5 for examples of peer coaching questions.

STEP 5: CONFIRM

Facilitator confirms where the member wants mentoring support.

STEP 6: MENTOR

Members share experiences, observations, and insights to provide support to help, but don't give prescriptive recommendations or advice.

STEP 7: REFLECT

The member being coached can now share their feedback and reactions to the experience (but not on the individual feedback given).

Downloads at-a-Glance

Visit www.grassrootsleadershipbook.com to download all the templates and materials mentioned in this book.

Chapter	Downloads available
3	Tips for running virtual groups
4	Confidentiality agreement "Getting to know you" exercises and debrief tips Session agenda
5	Powerful peer coaching questions Peer coach facilitator play-by-play Accountability template Session agenda
6	Accountability template Session agenda
8	Values worksheet Stop, start, continue worksheet Accountability template Session agenda
9	Strengths worksheet Accountability template Session agenda
10	Brand survey Brand statement boosters Accountability template Session agenda
11	Visioning exercise Accountability template Session agenda

Books to Read and Discuss Together

Personal Effectiveness

The Gifts of Imperfection by Brené Brown
Linchpin: Are You Indispensable? by Seth Godin
MOJO by Marshall Goldsmith
The No Asshole Rule by Robert Sutton
The Purpose Effect by Dan Pontefract
Quiet: The Power of Introverts in a World That Can't Stop Talking
     by Susan Cain
StrengthsFinder 2.0 by Tom Rath
Talent is Overrated by Geoff Colvin
Taming Your Gremlin by Rick Carson
What Got You Here Won't Get You There by Marshall Goldsmith

Productivity & Effectiveness

18 Minutes by Peter Bregman
Eat That Frog! by Brian Tracy
The First 90 Days by Michael Watkins
Getting Things Done by David Allen
The Power of Habit: Why We Do What We Do in Life and Business
     by Charles Duhigg

Communication

Crucial Conversations by Kerry Patterson et al
Fierce Conversations by Susan Scott
How to Win Friends and Influence People by Dale Carnegie
Influencer by Kerry Patterson et al
Made to Stick by Chip and Dan Heath
You Can't NOT Communicate 2 by David Grossman

Decision-Making & Problem-Solving

10-10-10 by Suzy Welch
the dip by Seth Godin
Paradox of Choice by Barry Schwartz
Six Thinking Hats by Edward de Bono

Creativity & Innovation

The Creative Habit by Twyla Tharp
Innovation and Entrepreneurship by Peter F. Drucker
Myths of Innovation by Scott Berkun
Stoking Your Innovation Bonfire by Braden Kelley
A Whole New Mind by Daniel Pink

Negotiation & Change Leadership

3-D Negotiation by David A. Lax and James K. Sebeniu
Bargaining For Advantage by G. Richard Shell
Change with Confidence by Phil Buckley
Getting to Yes by Roger Fisher, William L. Ury and Bruce Patton
Negotiation Genius by Deepak Malhotra and Max H. Baxerman

Strategy & Execution

Blue Ocean Strategy by W. Chan Kim and Renée Mauborgne
The Discipline of Market Leaders by Michael Treacy and Fred Wiersma
Good to Great by Jim Collins
The Lean Startup by Eric Ries
The One Page Business Plan by Jim Horan
Onward by Howard Schultz
Start with Why by Simon Sinek

Management & Leadership

The Coaching Habit by Michael Bungay Stanier
Dare to Lead by Brené Brown
The Essential Drucker by Peter F. Drucker
Fierce Leadership by Susan Scott
First, Break All The Rules by Marcus Buckingham & Curt Coffman
Judgment by Noel Tichy & Warren Bennis Finance
Leadership & Self Deception by The Arbinger Institute
The Leadership Challenge by James M. Kouzes and Barry Z. Posner
The New Leader's 100-Day Action Plan by George Bradt et al
Why Work Sucks and How to Fix it by Cali Ressler and
    Jody Thompson

Motivation & Team Development

Crush It! Why Now is the Time to Cash in on Your Passion by Gary
    Vaynerchuk
Drive by Daniel H. Pink
The Five Dysfunctions of a Team by Patrick Lencioni
The Good Fight by Liane Davey
Maverick: The Success Story Behind the World's Most Unusual
Screw it, Let's Do it by Richard Branson

Tribes: We Need You to Lead Us by Seth Godin
Workplace by R. Semler

Video Sources for Discussion & Learning

Coursera – https://www.coursera.org/
Goalcast – https://www.goalcast.com/
Mindvalley – https://www.mindvalley.com/
TED Talks – www.ted.com

Sources

Chapter 1

UNC Executive Development. "The Origen's of VUCA." UNC Executive Development Blog (website). March 10, 2017. http://execdev.kenan-flagler.unc.edu/blog/the-origins-of-vuca

Johansen, Bob. *The New Leadership Literacies: Thriving in a Future of Extreme Disruption and Distributed Everything.* Berrett-Koehler Publishers, 2017.

Watkins, Michael. *The First 90 Days, Updated and Expanded: Proven Strategies for Getting Up to Speed Faster and Smarter.* Harvard Business Review Press, 2013.

Chapter 2

Murthy, Vivek. "Work and the Loneliness Epidemic: Reducing Isolation at Work is Good for Business." *Harvard Business Review.* https://hbr.org/cover-story/2017/09/work-and-the-loneliness-epidemic

Chapter 3

Tuckman, Bruce W. "Developmental Sequence in Small Groups." Psychological Bulletin. 63 (6): 384–399, 1965.

Chapter 5

Dominican University of California. "Study Focuses on Strategies for Achieving Goals, Resolutions." Dominican University of California (website). https://www.dominican.edu/dominicannews/study-highlights-strategies-for-achieving-goals

Conclusion

Eisenberger, Naomi, Matthew Lieberman, and Kipling Williams. "Does Rejection Hurt? An FMRI Study of Social Exclusion." University of California, Los Angeles, 2003.

Acknowledgements

S O MANY PEOPLE have shaped this book and made it a reality. My journey in leadership began with my first boss, Jim Orban, who gave me my first break and, years later, continued to be generous in sharing his leadership journey with our Roundtable community. Thanks for not hanging up on me when I called you every day for two weeks for a job, Jim. I appreciate it!

I genuinely love and am fascinated by the art of leadership. Every leader I worked for taught me something about leadership. Some taught me who I wanted to be, and others taught me who I wanted to avoid being. All left an impression, but none more so than Don McQuaig, my boss, mentor, and friend from MICA. I will be forever grateful for the opportunity I had to work with Don. He taught me to see people's strengths, to be open to differences, to maintain high standards, and to love what you do. I miss his encouragement and hope that I've brought a little bit of the MICA spirit into the work we do at The Roundtable.

To my incredible team (past and present) at The Round-table, thank you for your unfailing support and belief—for challenging my thinking, for loving the work we do as much as I do, and for caring so much about our Roundtable community. When I look around our team I'm often amazed at how lucky I am to work with such incredible people who dream big, make an impact, have fun, and, more than anything else, know how to get shit done.

In the beginning, there was just an idea and a handful of people who believed in what I was trying to do. To Trish Hewitt, Mary Duncan, Tracey Rehel, Dave Moncur, Kathy Rethy, and Gabriella O'Rourke: thank you for your early support and advocacy. You will always be honorary members of The Roundtable. And to the indomitable Anna Petosa: thank you for being our first paying client. Thank you for always being open to trying out my crazy ideas, and thank you for always being there to lend an ear, a shoulder to cry on, and a stiff drink to bitch over. That bust of you for The Roundtable office is on order.

And to all of our members, thank you for being a part of the extended Roundtable tribe. We are growing bigger and stronger each and every year.

To the incredible team at Page Two, I can't thank you enough for your kind support, gentle pushing, and overall encouragement that got me to the finish line of this book. To Amanda Lewis and Trena White in particular—thank you for reframing my thinking and helping me get my millions of thoughts out clearly and (somewhat) succinctly. You are both masterful at your craft, and I am forever grateful.

Finally, and most importantly of all, to my husband D'Arcy McCabe, none of this would have happened without your support. Thank you for encouraging me to quit my fulltime job (despite the risks that meant for our family), and to take the headlong leap into self-employment. Thank you for believing that I could do it, even when I doubted myself. And to my darling daughter, Nia, I hope that seeing your mom do what she loves inspires you to pursue your dreams and live the life that you're meant to live. I love you both with all my heart.

About the Author

GLAIN (PRONOUNCED GLINE like SHINE) ROBERTS-MCCABE is the founder and president of The Roundtable, a company where leaders cultivate their leadership, together.

The Roundtable is best known for their peer coaching and mentoring systems that help organizations break down silos, increase collaboration, and accelerate business all while helping ambitious leaders navigate changes, disruption, and rapid growth.

In 2014, The Roundtable was awarded a Gold Award by the Canadian Awards for Training Excellence for their peer coaching and mentoring program, and in 2016 they were named Best External Consulting Advisory at the Canadian HR Awards. In 2018, Glain was named one of Canada's top women entrepreneurs at the RBC Canadian Women Entrepreneur Awards.

Glain believes that leadership is a privilege. Her personal mission is to inspire leaders to connect to their bigger purpose and passion so that work can be more fun, and life can be more fulfilling.

↓ Learn more about The Roundtable by visiting www.goroundtable.com

Interested in learning more about our work?

About The Roundtable

We're an organization committed to helping ambitious leaders navigate change, disruption and growth by building their coaching and collaboration skills. Check out our website to learn more about our programs for organizations and individuals. **Visit www.goroundtable.com.**

About The Group Coaching Academy

Interested in upping your group coaching skills? We've got you covered. The Group Coaching Academy helps coaches, trainers, and consultants build their group coaching capabilities and create group coaching programs that deliver impact. **Visit www.groupcoachacademy.com** to learn more and sign up for our tip sheet on creating group coaching programs that work.

Did I REALLY Sign Up for This?!? Book and Keynotes

Grab copies of Glain Roberts-McCabe's first book jammed with lessons learned, tested approaches, and leadership strategies culled from over two decades of leading and working with the best and brightest leaders from across sectors.

And, if you're looking to add a practical punch to your next leadership conference, book Glain on a variety of straight-ahead leadership topics. **Email info@goroundtable.com** for more details.

"I just found my new Brené Brown!"
CSAE 2019 Annual Conference attendee

www.ingramcontent.com/pod-product-compliance
Lightning Source LLC
Chambersburg PA
CBHW030516210326
41597CB00013B/933